Feeding the Crisis

CALIFORNIA STUDIES IN FOOD AND
CULTURE

Darra Goldstein, Editor

We used to go to the foodbank

Feeding the Crisis

*Care and Abandonment in
America's Food Safety Net*

Maggie Dickinson

UNIVERSITY OF CALIFORNIA PRESS

University of California Press, one of the most
distinguished university presses in the United States,
enriches lives around the world by advancing scholarship
in the humanities, social sciences, and natural sciences. Its
activities are supported by the UC Press Foundation and
by philanthropic contributions from individuals and
institutions. For more information, visit www.ucpress.edu.

University of California Press
Oakland, California

Library of Congress Cataloging-in-Publication Data

Names: Dickinson, Maggie, author.
Title: Feeding the crisis : care and abandonment in
    America's food safety net / Maggie Dickinson.
Other titles: California studies in food and culture ; 71.
Description: Oakland, California : The University of
    California Press, [2020] | Series: California studies in
    food and culture ; 71 | Includes bibliographical
    references and index.
Identifiers: LCCN 2019023235 (print) | LCCN 2019023236
    (ebook) | ISBN 9780520307667 (cloth) |
    ISBN 9780520307674 (paperback) |
    ISBN 9780520973770 (ebook)
Subjects: LCSH: Food relief—New York (State)—
    New York. | Food relief —Case studies—21st century.
    | Food relief—Government policy—United States. |
    Food security—New York (State)—New York.
Classification: LCC HV696.F6 D488 2020 (print) |
    LCC HV696.F6 (ebook) | DDC 363.809747/1 —dc23
LC record available at https://lccn.loc.gov/2019023235
LC ebook record available at https://lccn.loc.
    gov/2019023236

Manufactured in the United States of America

29 28 27 26 25 24 23 22 21 20
10 9 8 7 6 5 4 3 2 1

CONTENTS

ACKNOWLEDGMENTS

This research would not have been possible without the many North Brooklyn residents who shared their time, ideas, and experiences with me. Most important were my friends at the North Brooklyn Pantry, who welcomed me with open arms, especially Katrina, Ada, Lucy, Helena, Sunshine, Christine, Jen, and Ann. Though they are rarely recognized for the work they do, these women are the backbone of their communities. The world would be worse off without them and the many people like them who do the daily labor of making sure people are cared for. They are humble heroes.

I am grateful for the community of scholars who have supported this research over many years. This book is far better thanks to the steadfast support of Leith Mullings, whose wisdom and commitment to social justice are a constant source of inspiration. Jeff Maskovsky, Frances Fox Piven, and Julie Guthman offered invaluable insights on early iterations of this work. Jan Poppendieck's research has been foundational to my own. She has become a mentor, collaborator, and friend in the years since she graciously agreed to read my first research proposal. Special thanks go to Karen Williams, who has probably read every word I've ever written at least twice and whose friendship has made academia a much better place to be. Thanks to the many people who have read versions of this work at various stages and offered their insights on the project including Andrea Morrell, Javiela Evangelista, Sophie Bjork James, Risa Cromer, Daisy Deomampo, Ujju Agarwal, Victoria Lawson, Sarah Elwood, Anahi Viladrich, Harmony Goldberg, Preeti Sampat, Nazia Kazi, David Boarder Giles, Teresa Mares, Kara Dean Assael, Abby Dickinson, Pem Buck, Sherry Deckman, Tashana Samuels, Angelina Tallaj, Kandice Chuh, Mary Taylor, Francesca Manning, Christopher Loperena, Lorena Fuentes, Danford Chibvongodze, and Tony Lucero. I am also grateful for my colleagues at CUNY's Guttman Community College and for my students who give me hope that a better world is on its way.

I received support for this work through the Wenner Gren Foundation; the CUNY Faculty Fellowship Publication Program; the Center for Place, Culture and Politics; and The Relational Poverty Network's summer institute at the University of Washington. Kate Marshall saw the potential in this work early on. I am grateful for her steady advice and encouragement, which kept the project moving forward. I am also indebted to my manuscript reviewers, Alison Alkon and John Clarke. Alison's detailed feedback on the manuscript was an incredible gift that made this a much better book. The title *Feeding the Crisis* is in many ways an homage to the classic book *Policing the Crisis* and the kind of social, cultural, and political economic analysis it pioneered. It meant the world to me that John Clarke, one of the coauthors of that book, was so supportive of this one.

It is hard to imagine how this book could have come together without the help of so many caregivers who helped make the space and time for me to write. Thanks to my mother, Karen Dickinson; Mary Katherine Youngblood; Ora Yemini Morrison; Niseema Diemer; and the many teachers at JV Forrestal and Sargent Elementary schools.

James Case Leal has supported me every step of the way on this project. Thank you for your patience and your encouragement. I love you like a fact. This book is dedicated to Emmanuel and Diego, whom I love beyond words.

CHAPTER ONE

Feeding the Crisis

personal narrative

Nigel walked into the North Brooklyn Pantry on a hot summer day in the middle of July.[1] I was happy to see him. He was not happy to be back. I had been volunteering at the pantry every week for over a year. I had become part of a motley crew, made up mostly of older women who had lived in the neighborhood for decades. Fabiola, Angela, Katherine, and Ada had welcomed me into the fold, and together we did most of the day-to-day work of the pantry. We carried boxes of cans up the narrow, wooden steps from the basement to the pews upstairs and packed blue plastic bags with a random assortment of food from the food bank each week. We registered several hundred neighborhood residents, gave them each a bag of groceries, and managed conflicts as residents waiting on the line grew restless. We returned leftover food to the basement at the end of the day and cleaned up all the boxes and bits of packaging from the sanctuary floor so the church would be ready for services on Sunday.

volunteer

Nigel had joined our ragtag crew in February. He lived a few blocks away in a run-down single room that he shared with a roommate. He started coming to dinner at the North Brooklyn Pantry's soup kitchen on Tuesday nights and soon after began helping out at the pantry each week. Like Angela and Fabiola, two of the most dedicated and consistent volunteers, he relied heavily on the food he took with him from the pantry. All three had started out as pantry clients struggling with deep poverty before they became regular volunteers. Everyone appreciated Nigel. He worked hard, had a good sense of humor, and didn't mind lifting heavy boxes that the rest of us could barely manage. But we had not seen him for the past two months because he had started working as a bus boy at a diner in Manhattan. I could track his economic fortunes based on whether or not he showed up to volunteer. When he was working, he disappeared. When he lost a job, he came back.

Food assistance has become the leading edge of the twenty-first-century response to growing poverty and economic insecurity. Since the turn of the millennium, there has been an unprecedented outpouring of food assistance across the United States, encompassing both federally funded food programs like SNAP (formerly referred to as food stamps) and emergency food providers like soup kitchens and food pantries.[2] During the George W. Bush administration, national food stamp rolls rose from just above eighteen million in 2001 to twenty-seven million in 2008. This growth gained even more momentum as a deep recession took hold. By the end of 2012, the rolls reached a record forty-seven million Americans, or around 15 percent of the US population. Despite an official economic recovery, SNAP rolls remain near this historic high, serving over forty-two million people in 2017 (United States Department of Agriculture 2018). The number of people served by soup kitchens and food pantries in this same period has also risen, from twenty-five million rise in people served at soup kitchens

in 2005 to 46.5 million in 2012 (Wienfield et al. 2014, Malbi et al. 2010). Millions of American households rely on these forms of food assistance to make ends meet each month. In pantries and soup kitchens across the country, thousands of volunteers show up week after week to cook meals and serve groceries to people in need. And yet, despite a massively expanded food safety net, more than forty-one million Americans experienced food insecurity in 2016 (Coleman-Jensen et al. 2017).

The conventional wisdom is that welfare programs have been continually cut back and systematically dismantled both in the United States and globally since the 1980s. But the expansion of food assistance tells a different story—and a more accurate one. In fact, welfare state spending in the United States—and especially programs targeted to poor households—has been growing since the mid-1980s (Moffitt 2015). The growth of the food safety net mirrors larger transitions in the ways policy makers have chosen to address poverty and economic insecurity. The twenty-first-century safety net in the United States has expanded to manage growing poverty and insecurity but does little to alter the political and economic realities that create these conditions in the first place. Since the 1980s, wages for middle- and working-class workers have stagnated, low-wage jobs have proliferated, and work has become more insecure. In what Jacob Hacker has termed "the great risk shift," employers have walked away from their obligations—from providing full-time work and regular schedules to offering health care, pensions, and other protections to the people who work for them (Hacker 2006, Lambert 2008). Families across the United States have experienced an ongoing housing crisis, marked by foreclosures and evictions (Desmond 2016), adding to a sense of instability and uncertainty for many Americans. As jobs have become more

welfare growing

instability of work, health care is increasing

insecure and the cost of living has increased, food assistance has quietly expanded to meet a growing need.

Instead of fixing the crisis of growing economic precarity and insecurity, we are feeding it. Pantry clients and volunteers, like Nigel, Angela, and Fabiola, are on the front lines of a new kind of safety net made up of a complicated patchwork of generosity and withholding, care and abandonment. Programs like SNAP have been reconfigured to subsidize low-wage workers who do not earn enough at their jobs to afford basic necessities like food. SNAP is a federal program that provides funds to low-income households that can be used to purchase food at grocery stores and other retailers. The program has been rebranded as a "work support," and low-wage workers are encouraged to enroll in the program by policy makers as well as sometimes even their employers (Adad-Santos 2013). At the same time, federal funding for public-private partnerships has unleashed a massive expansion of community groups and nonprofits working to address hunger. The growing network of emergency food providers (EFPs) is comprised of regional food banks that distribute food to small, local community organizations like soup kitchens and food pantries that primarily operate out of faith-based organizations. As Jan Poppendieck points out, EFPs distribute food as charity and, unlike SNAP, offer clients "no enforceable rights whatsoever" (Poppendieck 1994). Both forms of food assistance have expanded dramatically since the turn of the millennium and have become an interlocking system governing hunger and food insecurity in new ways. People like Nigel rely on both forms of food assistance, turning from one to the other depending on changes in their circumstances.

Nigel was forty years old when we met—an African American Marine veteran who had worked in restaurants for most of his adult life. His easy-going outlook made him the black sheep in his family. He grew up in a middle-class home in Brooklyn. His dad was an office worker in a large corporation. His sister had a law degree. Nigel chose a different path, but it wasn't a particularly troubled one. He had no criminal record and no complicated family life. He never married, had no children, and expressed no regrets about these choices. As a self-described free spirit, Nigel wasn't rich, but he had always managed to hold down an apartment and a job. He saw himself as "a regular guy" who liked to work and was satisfied with life.

His regular life began to unravel in 2011, when his Brooklyn apartment building was condemned and he was forced to move. This was the first in a series of crises that would plague Nigel for the next three years. At the time, he was working as a sous chef in a small Brooklyn restaurant. He realized it would be a long time until he would be able to save enough to get a place of his own. After wearing out his welcome on a friend's couch, he went into the New York City shelter system, which placed him in a housing facility in the Bronx. It was a two-hour commute to his job in Brooklyn, and his late-night work hours conflicted with the curfew at the housing facility. Eventually, he was fired for leaving work early one too many times in order to make it back to the Bronx to have a bed to sleep in. The restaurant had been paying him off the books, so he couldn't apply for unemployment insurance when he lost his job. He found himself with no home, no money, and no way to get back on his feet.

Nigel was miserable in the shelter. He was living in an unfamiliar neighborhood under strict rules that he found constraining. After nearly six months, his counselor there managed to get him transferred to a single-room-occupancy building near the North Brooklyn Pantry. There was no curfew, so he would be able to come and go as he pleased and set his own schedule. One of the requirements of his new housing was that he open a public assistance case so he could qualify for the $215 rent subsidy, a small cash allowance, and food stamps. Nigel had never applied for food stamps or public assistance before. He was grateful to have the help while he looked for work, but he was also uneasy. "Sure, I paid my taxes, I did service for the country, but a year ago, I wasn't in the system. I didn't know I could apply for ... I never even knew about this stuff. How to get SNAP and all this stuff. And my eyes are still being opened. It's an education, but I'm not quite sure I want the degree. I want to start working again. I want to be regular again. I want to be a regular guy. I really do. But I'm here and I can't really pull that off quite yet." Between public assistance, food stamps, soup kitchens, and food from the pantry, Nigel made ends meet while he looked for work. He eventually landed a job at a diner, which paid minimum wage. He was happy to be working again. The other volunteers at the pantry hoped he would finally be able to get back on his feet. However, the job did not pay enough to really change his situation. He still qualified for food stamps, and saving for an apartment would be a challenge. But it was a job, and it meant at least he no longer needed food from the pantry.

Then, after two months, Nigel's boss decided to take him off the books and pay him $5 an hour plus tips. Nigel, an experienced restaurant worker, balked at the request. "He wanted to take me off the books because I was making *too much* on minimum wage." It wasn't just the pay cut that bothered Nigel. It was also the fact that he would no longer receive paystubs or tax forms. Working under the table would mean he would no longer qualify for the wage subsidies provided to low-wage workers, including the earned income tax credit, credit toward unem-

employers paycost— results in worker not

ployment, and social security. Being paid off the books meant he would lose his food stamp benefits as well. Single adults are required to show they work twenty hours a week in exchange for food assistance—something that is hard to prove without documentation. As Nigel put it, "I need something on paper. I want a paper trail now. I need my taxes. I need my refund. I really do." Nigel was dejected by the whole situation. He quit, hoping he could find something better. "I'm walking home (from work) with forty, fifty bucks, which is something, but I thought I should be treated better. So, I left. I walked out. In retrospect, perhaps I should have at least stayed to see how that would have played out. But I didn't. What's the saying? Pride before fall? So therefore, I fell."

When Nigel left his job, he lost his food stamps because he could no longer show that he was working. He returned to the food pantry and the soup kitchen as his main source of sustenance. He was frustrated by his lack of work, low pay, and unstable housing. We worked side by side that afternoon, and after several hours of sorting cans and packing bags, he left, taking rice, canned peas, apple juice, and some day-old bread from a local bakery with him. Like many of the people who came to the pantry, Nigel needed help finding a job and stable, affordable housing, but what he found instead was food. Every crisis was met with a bag of groceries or a hot meal.

Nigel's experience raises some important questions about the contemporary response to poverty in the United States. Why have these entangled economic crises been met with the outpouring of *food*? What is the particular historical and political climate that has made expanding food assistance the preferred remedy for stagnating wages, widespread un- and underemployment, and growing precarity and insecurity for the working class? And what does this expansion of food assistance in the twenty-first century mean for the ways we can, collectively, imagine addressing the economic crises and insecurities of the present moment?

WHY FOOD?

Understanding the growth of the food safety net requires an understanding of the broader political context in which food has become the go-to solution to poverty in the twenty-first century. The growth in the food safety net is linked to three major developments, which I lay out in more detail below and in the chapters that follow: a fundamental transformation of the US welfare state in the late twentieth century, the emergence of public-private partnerships as a primary solution to issues of poverty, and growing concerns about obesity and diet-related disease.

Welfare reforms passed in the mid-1990s garnered a tremendous amount of scholarly and political attention. These reforms sharply restricted access to cash assistance for poor families with children in the United States, giving rise to the political common sense that both political parties in the United States were committed to shrinking the size and scope of the welfare state as a whole. Mainstream political analysts have largely celebrated the reduction in cash assistance as an unqualified success, reducing both spending and the role of government in the lives of the poor. On the left, analysts have linked welfare reforms with a broader process of impoverishment and growing income inequality through restricted access to aid, including a startling rise in extreme poverty in the United States (Maskovsky and Morgen 2003, Piven 2001, Edin and Shaefer 2016). Social theorists

contraction of
cash
benefits

have argued that cuts to cash assistance represent "the continual contraction of welfare in the age of hypermobile capital and flexible work"(Wacquant 2009). Others show how politicians built support for cuts to cash assistance for poor families by mobilizing thinly veiled racial stereotypes about welfare recipients. In the process, they successfully inflamed racial divisions over the role of the social safety net in society, making racism the single most important factor driving white Americans' opposition to welfare (Gilens 1999).

What has been largely overlooked in much of this analysis is the degree to which social spending targeted to the poor has, in fact, grown. While unemployed single-parent households have less access to public benefits, employed, two-parent households have much more access to assistance today (Ben-Shalom, Moffitt, and Scholz 2011; Moffitt 2015). In the early 2000s, policy makers at the federal, state, and local levels began to ease access to food stamp benefits. These efforts were largely motivated by a new attitude among administrators and policy makers that reframed food stamps as a "work support" for low-wage workers. The expansion of food stamps fit the mold of safety-net programs, such as the earned income tax credit, that subsidize wages and exclude non-workers from assistance. Politicians no longer rely on overt racial stereotypes like the infamous welfare queen to argue for cuts to social programs. Instead, they have redesigned the social safety net to benefit low-income workers, who are framed as deserving because they work. At the same time, these policies exclude a growing population of unemployed or informally employed residents, associating them with the long-standing racialized stereotype of the lazy, undeserving poor. Non-workers are fast becoming a distinct group who can be cut out of the social compact and excluded from social protections.

This new welfare state configuration, subsidizing low-wage workers and excluding the unemployed or informally employed, is the template on which future budget decisions will likely be made. As the Trump administration's budget director, Mick Mulvaney, recently put it, "If you are on food stamps and you are able bodied, we need you to go to work. There is a dignity to work and there's a necessity to work to help the country succeed"(Purser and Hennigan 2017). The Trump administration's push to tighten the links between SNAP assistance and work is part of a broader project to link all forms of public assistance, including Medicaid, to participation in the labor force. Nigel's experience is typical. Losing his job meant losing his SNAP benefits because he could no longer show that he was employed. By tying food stamps to work, these benefits have become a key incentive and a key punishment, encouraging working people to accept the increasingly poor terms employers are offering them. At a political level, distinctions between the working poor and the non-working poor have become a racializing discourse, justifying the exclusion of a group of citizens from basic rights and protections, like the right to food or health care.[3]

As I show in chapters 2 and 3, reorienting welfare assistance around the idea of "work support" also has radical implications for the gender dimensions of the twenty-first-century welfare state. Chapter 2 looks at how programs that once primarily assisted poor mothers in the care of their children now support poor workers in their ability to work. I follow two mothers, Nydia and Adwa, as they navigate SNAP policies that determine which families have access to food assistance and which do not. Women gain access to food assistance by performing the role of the "good mother." However, good mothering, under these policies, has been redefined as providing a role model for children by going to work and holding down a job.

In chapter 3, I show how the work-based safety net complicates assumptions about men, fatherhood, and welfare. Welfare policy in the United States was designed around the ideal of the wage-earning male who worked to provide for his dependents. In an era of insecure work, this ideal is increasingly out of reach for many poor and working-class men. Through the experiences of two men, Jimmy and Jesús, who regularly frequented the North Brooklyn Pantry, chapter 3 shows how men use food assistance to fulfill their roles as caregivers within their family networks. Their experiences challenge the narrative that welfare programs enable absentee fathers to abandon their children, suggesting instead that food assistance is a way for men to maintain family ties in the absence of well-paid work.

The second development shaping the growing food safety net is the heavy investment in public-private partnerships and the emphasis on voluntary or private efforts to address poverty. The growth and institutionalization of food banks, soup kitchens, and food pantries is part of a significant push toward states contracting out social services to nonprofit service agencies, a process that began in the 1960s in the United States and more recently in Europe (Muehlebach 2011, Ranci 2001, Crenson and Ginsberg 2002). The role of the state is no longer to provide people with social protections but to encourage private citizens and local organizations to take responsibility for poverty and other social problems. Emergency food providers began growing rapidly in the 1980s and today engage an enormous number of volunteers (Poppendieck 1998). Like other nonprofits that are contracted to provide social services, EFPs "expand the welfare state without expanding the state itself" (Crenson and Ginsberg

2002, 225). Feeding America, the national umbrella organization that supports and promotes food banks in the United States, boasts that "food banks combine USDA commodities and storage and distribution funding with private donations of food and funds, infrastructure, and manpower to leverage the program far beyond its budgeted amount. In this way, the USDA and the emergency food system exemplify an optimum model of public-private partnership" (2018).

Previous expansions of welfare benefits have made the state a target of collective political action for poor people demanding access to more resources. In the 1960s, a powerful national welfare rights movement emerged out of the broader civil rights movements (Piven and Cloward 1979, Nadasen 2004, Kornbluh 2007, West 1981). Activists sat in at welfare offices and pushed for legislation that would expand support for the work that poor women did as mothers and caretakers in their communities. Expansions of the welfare state through contracting out to non-profit organizations make these kinds of collective political actions less likely, since the public face of emergency food providers is not a street-level government bureaucrat whose job depends, at least to some degree, on serving clients, but a volunteer. In this way, the growth of nonprofit social service providers is a key aspect of contemporary poverty governance, replacing entitlements provided by the state with charity. Unlike state-provided welfare benefits, social services that are contracted out provide resources without expanding rights. As Jeff Maskovsky and Judith Goode have shown, this form of privatization, "removes the poor from a direct relationship with the state, a relationship that historically has been essential to the expression of collective agency for poor communities. In this context, the neoliberal celebration of the removal of the state from poor people's everyday lives may be seen for what it is: an ideological power play" (Maskovsky and Goode 2001, 9).

A central component of public-private partnerships, in contrast to traditional state-run welfare programs, is mobilizing an enormous volunteer labor force that can carry out the work of distributing food aid for little or no compensation. Chapter 4 provides an analysis of the new labor regimes emerging out of the growing emergency food network. As emergency food providers like soup kitchens and food pantries proliferate across the country, these institutions have become an important site of informal employment. Poor women who volunteer, like Fabiola and Angela, are empowered to care for their communities. Chapter 4 also examines how all caring labor, including volunteer work, is shaped by race, class, and gender inequalities and explores the conflicts that emerge around how volunteer labor in emergency food providers should be remunerated, recognized, and regulated.

The final development driving the expansion of federal food assistance is growing concern about obesity and diet-related illnesses like diabetes and heart disease that disproportionately impact poor people. Food aid has increasingly been linked to debates about obesity, nutrition, public health, and urban health inequalities.[4] Nearly 10 percent of American adults suffer from diabetes, and 32 percent have high blood pressure (CDC 2018, 2017). Living in poverty significantly increases people's chances of developing these conditions and suffering more serious complications from them (Kim, Berger, and Matte 2006). Growing concerns over the links between poverty and chronic diet-related disease have led policy makers to put public health concerns at the center of food policy.

Policy makers and advocates emphasize the importance of programs like SNAP and emergency food to encourage healthy eating. Chronic illnesses such as diabetes, heart disease, and hypertension are consistently described in market terms: as a cost to the overall economy in direct medical expenses, lost productivity, higher insurance premiums, and absence from work. The fear is no longer that poor people in the United States might go hungry. It is that without food assistance, they will eat poorly, get sick, and become a costly burden on society. In recent congressional debates over cuts to the SNAP program, Representative Jim McGovern put it succinctly, "a cut of $2 billion a year in food stamps could trigger an increase in $15 billion in medical costs for diabetes over the next decade.... Any cuts will cost us more. They will save us nothing" (McGovern 2014). Policy makers have maintained strong support for SNAP as both a work support and as a nutrition program necessary for maintaining a viable, healthy labor force in the United States. And yet improvements in low-income households' health remain elusive.

Chapter 5 shows how the increased attention to health and nutrition in the food safety net has not translated into significantly improved nutrition outcomes for poor families. Stephanie's experience shows how poor families make do in the face of bureaucratic neglect from the welfare office, SNAP policies designed to keep people on the edge of food insecurity, a food system where the cheapest calories are also the unhealthiest, and unreliable resources from food pantries. As she and her husband struggle to find work, maintain their housing, and feed their children, they experience long periods of severe food insecurity. Over the course of a year, Stephanie's health deteriorates, posing new challenges as she attempts to secure work that can halt her family's downward spiral into deep poverty. Her experience demonstrates the inadequacies of the current food safety net as a public health intervention.

These three developments all point to a transformation in the relationship between the state, the labor market, and citizens. Since the 1980s, the rollback of the regulatory state has led to rising inequality and insecurity. The role of the safety net is no longer to protect citizens from economic misfortune, but to create the optimal conditions for companies and individuals to act in ways that promote economic growth. State policies are designed to cajole individuals into "productivity"—through work, through community service, and through optimizing their health. Antipoverty policy is being used to grease the wheels of labor exploitation—not only by cutting assistance to poor families (Piven 2001, Peck 2001), but also by expanding it in ways that subsidize low-wage work, encourage community organizations to take responsibility for poverty, and help individuals maintain work-ready bodies.

To a remarkable extent, food assistance in the United States has been transformed to support the employment relationship and to cut costs—not to ensure that poor people have access to food. When people like Nigel lose a job, they are often cut off from federal food assistance and turn to emergency food providers like soup kitchens and food pantries. This configuration of assistance represents a shift from the way welfare state programs operated in the twentieth century. Welfare protections were extended in the postwar era largely in response to social movements (Piven and Cloward 1993). The programs that were created safeguarded people from certain predictable risks, such as illness, old age, or unemployment caused by dips in the business cycle. But the relationship between these programs and the labor market has shifted significantly. In an era when work has become flexible, insecure, and unreliable, the predictable risks have changed. With low-wage, part-time jobs becoming more prevalent in the United States, social support is being transformed to protect against the systemic risk of below-subsistence wages and to punish and exclude poor people who fail to establish a foothold in the formal economy. Thus, the growing food safety net is, in many ways, a set of technocratic fixes to the problems of economic insecurity, based in policies designed to push people into the labor market rather than to protect them when the market fails. The urgent need is for new politics and policies that can address both hunger and economic insecurity. Chapter 6 draws on the insights and analyses of the people profiled in this book to suggest a new approach to anti-hunger politics that does just that.

SEEING POWER

This study is based on two years of ethnographic research in the North Brooklyn Pantry. In addition to helping out around the pantry, I held regular hours each week to assist people applying for public benefits, including SNAP. I went to the welfare office with them and read through the inscrutable letters from New York City's Human Resources Administration, trying to help make sense of the convoluted legalese that often meant the difference between having money for food or rent and getting mired in an even deeper financial crisis. My interest was initially in food programs, but I quickly realized that food was often just the tip of the iceberg. I sought out local advocates and nonprofits to find programs that could assist people in finding jobs and housing. As much as I tried, I never found a jobs program that could successfully connect pantry clients with decent work. Housing advocates I spoke to pointed to temporary housing options. The only permanent possibility was public housing, but the waiting list was decades long. The need for permanent, affordable housing in New York far outweighs the availability. There were simply no effective programs for connecting people with affordable housing or decent jobs. What I could almost always do, however, was help people get food, either in the form of a pantry bag or through a SNAP application.

While other ethnographic researchers attempt to "intervene as little as possible" (Desmond 2016, 321) in order to observe life as it is actually lived, my approach was based on interfering. I argued with welfare workers, asked pointed questions, and helped community members prepare their documents so that they would more easily qualify for benefits. I learned the ins and outs of how to do this work from a network of citywide advocates who had been pushing to expand access to food stamps in New York City for many years. I also conducted two focus groups with case workers at the welfare offices in North Brooklyn and interviewed nine local pantry directors, who are often the gatekeepers of food assistance. Eleanor Leacock has argued that, "given an able and conscientious researcher, advocacy leads to a fuller and more accurate understanding than attempted neutrality" (Leacock 1987). Advocacy can lead to theoretical insights because it can uncover how power works in everyday interactions. Starting from the assumption that poverty and food insecurity are not natural conditions but the product of political choices, I wanted to understand the barriers people encountered in their attempts to secure food. As Phillipe Bourgois has argued, "the best way to document the inadequacy of social services is to . . . assist, accompany and document"(Bourgois 2011, 4).

The core of my ethnographic work was as an advocate and resource for individuals in their dealings with the welfare office.

But unlike Bourgois in his study of homeless heroin addicts, I did not confine my research to people who are often perceived as the most abject residents of the city. Though many of the people I met and interviewed were homeless and struggled with addiction, others were barely clinging to a middle-class lifestyle. Because I conducted interviews and participant observation with a range of community residents, my findings are essentially comparative. I was able to detect patterns in people's treatment, their ability to access welfare benefits, and their access to food assistance. In doing so, I document not only the inadequacy of social services, but also the adequacy—the people for whom social services work quite well.

What I found was that the growing food safety net is entirely compatible with, and even enforces, large-scale changes in the economy, including the expansion of the low-wage labor force and the abandonment of a growing class of socially and economically marginal citizens. Welfare and work are often portrayed as polar opposites in contemporary popular discourse, with work being revered as dignified and worthy and welfare being scorned as it's opposite, breeding dependency and sloth. However, ethnographers have long demonstrated the interdependence of work and welfare in the lives and economic survival strategies of the poor, blurring stark distinctions between welfare "dependents" and those who work (Lein and Edin 1997, Newman 1999, Stack 1974, Scharff 1987). Though the welfare reforms of 1996 promised to end welfare as we knew it, they did not, in fact, end welfare. These reforms did, however, significantly reshape the relationship between work, welfare, citizens, and the state.

The people I met over the course of this research navigated a complicated system of welfare programs, formal jobs, informal employment, and charity to make ends meet. Changes in their circumstances had profound effects on whether and what they could eat. Tracking these changing circumstances over time revealed the new contours of deservingness and abandonment that shape the twenty-first-century welfare state. Poor New Yorkers like Nigel, Fabiola, and Angela navigated this complicated patchwork of resources day in and day out. Their very lives depend on the kinds of resources they can cobble together out of what's left of the safety net, a labor market that provides little in the way of security or sufficiency, and an enormous network of charitable food programs that provide resources without rights. What emerged as I accompanied them and assisted them in their efforts to feed themselves and their families, was a safety net designed to manage poverty and hunger—not to end it.

This book tells the stories of eight families living in North Brooklyn who turn to food assistance to make ends meet. I chose to carry out this research in New York City because it was one of the only places in the country that imposed food stamp work requirements in the wake of the Great Recession. In New York, the Bloomberg administration chose to enforce a rule that food stamp recipients who are not elderly, disabled, or caring for a child prove that they are working at least twenty hours a week or risk being cut off from their SNAP benefits. At the time, New York was an outlier in terms of food assistance policy. However, as the unemployment rate has fallen across the nation, many states have either opted in or been required by the USDA to enforce SNAP work requirements. Congressional Republicans have attempted to tighten work requirements for SNAP since the 2012 Farm Bill negotiations. The Trump administration has recently encouraged states and federal agencies to expand work requirements for Medicaid, and housing assistance as well, making New York City an important test case for what will happen across the country as these policies continue to be pursued at the national level.

Though areas in New York like the South Bronx have some of the highest rates of food insecurity in the nation, I was not interested in telling an exceptional story. Instead, I wanted to see what food insecurity looks like in an average community. Like the majority of food stamp recipients in the United States, the majority of residents in North Brooklyn are white. Given the ways welfare programs have been associated with people of color and poor single mothers and deployed as racist dog whistles (Haney-Lopez 2014, Gilens 1999), it was important to me to do this research in a community that matched the racial demographics of the nation as a whole.[5] The clients at the North Brooklyn Pantry and the residents I worked closely with came from a range of racial and ethnic backgrounds. Race and class certainly played a role in shaping both my relationship with community residents and people's experiences within the labor market, housing market, and their interactions with welfare offices (Soss, Fording, and Schram 2011; Massey and Denton 1993; DiTomaso 2013). White clients at the North Brooklyn Pantry were more likely to have family networks and resources they could draw on in the face of a personal economic crisis. They often had advantages built up over generations of access to better jobs, education, and housing that insulated them from some of the more degrading aspects of engaging with the welfare system and the housing and labor markets.

Ethnographers have long debated the impact of race, gender, and class on their ability to carry out research (Narayan 1993, Jacobs-Huey 2008). My role as a researcher and an educated white woman were moderated somewhat by two factors. The first was the connections I built with the regular volunteers at the pantry. As a mother of two young children and a poorly funded graduate student from a working-class background, I often had to bring my children with me to volunteer at the pantry. The women who ran the North Brooklyn Pantry doted on my children, and we built close relationships around our identities as mothers. Katherine, one of the regular volunteers, lived on the same block as my family. She took me under her wing, putting aside food from the pantry that she thought my children would like and keeping an eye on them while I conducted interviews and helped pantry clients with their SNAP applications. The second was my role as an advocate, which helped me to build trust with pantry clients and community residents who came to me in search of help with their benefits. Through the process of advocating on their behalf, I was able to corroborate their accounts with official documentation from the welfare office and in my everyday interactions with them at the food pantry.

Like any place, there are particularities unique to the North Brooklyn Pantry and the surrounding community. One of the primary factors impacting residents in North Brooklyn was gentrification and the skyrocketing price of housing. Though rising housing costs and housing insecurity are often causes of food insecurity, the rapid gentrification of North Brooklyn made housing a particularly acute problem for residents. Throughout the 1990s and 2000s, real estate developers converted the affordable—though often dilapidated—housing in the neighborhood into high-end apartments for wealthier tenants. As a result, many local residents experienced housing instability. They lost apartments to rent increases, harassment by landlords interested in renting to higher-income tenants, or the sale of buildings to developers for renovation. The housing crisis in North Brooklyn has pushed many low-income households into substandard living situations: doubled up in overcrowded apartments to make rent, relegated to homeless shelters, or living in rented rooms with little or no access to cooking facilities. These conditions significantly impact people's ability to prepare and store food, making them more likely to experience food insecurity. For many clients at the North Brooklyn Pantry, their struggles with food were intimately linked with their struggles for housing.

However, many of the barriers to economic security that the men and women at the North Brooklyn Pantry encountered were rooted in policies and decisions made at the national level and in broader economic trends that effect working-class residents across the United States. The ideology of work and reward has been enormously important for regulating the American labor market and American society in general. Its breakdown—the idea that work will no longer bring material rewards—is a tremendously unsettling force. Workers have been displaced en masse through the loss of manufacturing jobs, and this surplus labor force has been pushed into informal and entrepreneurial labor, with intense competition for the jobs that remain. In an era of economic restructuring and downward mobility, with falling wages and an increasing atmosphere of insecurity and doom, food assistance programs retooled as work supports and public health interventions do important political work. They buttress ideas of work and reward in ways that continue to divide the working class in the United States into a deserving poor worthy of care and an undeserving poor at risk of abandonment. The growing food safety net is redefining who deserves help and what form that help should come in—either as federal food assistance used to procure food at the grocery store or as charity from a soup kitchen or food pantry. Taken together, the expansion of this two-pronged food safety net helps to justify and further entrench the changes in the labor market that are driving the need for more food in the first place.

CHAPTER TWO

Care and Abandonment in the Food Safety Net

The expansion of food assistance in the twenty-first century—what I call today's growing food safety net—differs radically from the expansion of food assistance that took place in the 1970s, when the basic architecture of the modern food stamp program was put in place. The expansion of food assistance in the 1970s was one of the last major achievements of the War on Poverty. Spurred by the civil rights movement, the goal of the War on Poverty was to extend economic citizenship rights to all Americans, including African Americans who had been excluded from many of the New Deal welfare state programs established in the 1930s (Katznelson 2005, Quadagno 1996). The modern food stamp program emerged out of a deep-seated belief that hunger in a wealthy nation like the United States was intolerable and that the federal government had an obligation to make sure that no one starved.

In the late 1960s, Robert Kennedy embarked on a poverty tour to bring attention to pockets of severe poverty across the United States. In the Deep South and Appalachia, he and his team met listless children with clear signs of clinical malnutrition, including swollen bellies, wounds that would not heal, and stunted growth. Following in their footsteps, a team of doctors and nurses funded by the Field Foundation visited these same areas, documenting the prevalence of hunger and its terrible physical effects on children and others. They reported seeing children "suffering from hunger and disease, and directly or indirectly, … dying from them—which is exactly what 'starvation' means" (Robertson 1967). A separate investigation by the labor-backed Citizens Crusade Against Poverty identified 256 "hunger counties" across the United States. Attention to "the hunger issue" exploded when a 1968 CBS documentary titled *Hunger in America* brought these findings to the American people (Levenstein 1993).

Images of visibly malnourished children shocked many Americans. There was a sense of disbelief that such severe hunger could exist in what, at the time, was broadly considered an affluent society. Just a few years earlier Michael Harrington, in his unflinching expose of poverty in a land of plenty, had written, "To be sure, the other America is not impoverished in the same sense as those poor nations where millions cling to hunger as a defense against starvation. This country has escaped such extremes" (Harrington 1962). And yet the images emerging from Appalachia and the Deep South in the late 1960s provided stark proof that this was not the case. Not everyone living in the United States had, in fact, escaped such extremes.

The political response to these findings and the public concern they generated was swift and dramatic, largely because they emerged in a moment of high social movement activity. Poverty politics in the late 1960s was dominated by social movements like the National Welfare Rights Organization (NWRO) that were engaged in a national campaign to expand access to welfare and to institute a guaranteed income for all Americans (Nadasen 2004). By the late 1960s, leaders in the civil rights movement had shifted focus to winning economic rights through multiracial organizing efforts like the Poor People's Campaign. In this context, groups across the political spectrum were galvanized to push for political action on the hunger issue, which seemed like an intolerable manifestation of poverty. Civil rights activists who had long been involved in antipoverty struggles and welfare rights campaigns demanded changes to the food stamp program so that families with little or no cash could more easily access food assistance (Robertson 1967, Kornbluh 2015). Grassroots activists like the Black Panther Party took matters into their own hands by organizing programs of free breakfast for children and free groceries, building community support for their revolutionary political agenda and embarrassing the federal government into taking action (Nelson 2012, Patel 2012, 3).[1] Journalistic exposés on hunger proliferated and Congress quickly initiated its own investigations into the extent of the problem in the United States. Liberal advocacy groups formed and pushed Congress to take action. Hunger quickly emerged as an unavoidable political issue. Both Richard Nixon and Hubert Humphrey campaigned on promises to end hunger in the United States in the 1968 presidential election (Levenstein 1993, 150).

Under tremendous public pressure to address hunger and poverty, the Nixon administration and Congress moved swiftly to expand access to food assistance. By 1974, the food stamp program was available in all fifty states and the school lunch program had also been expanded (Levenstein 1993). The Food Stamp Act of 1977 finally eliminated the food stamp purchase requirement, which meant poor families no longer needed to have cash up front to purchase food stamps (Poppendieck 1998). The effect of these policy changes on hunger in the United States was dramatic. Enrollment in the food stamp program jumped from three million in 1969 to eighteen million in 1976 (United States Department of Agriculture 2018). Doctors who had documented the effects of severe hunger in the late 1960s revisited those same communities a decade later and found that clinical malnutrition had been virtually wiped out in the United States. The swollen bellies that were so prevalent a decade before were nowhere to be found. Researchers reported, "Where visitors ten years ago could quickly see large numbers of stunted, apathetic children with swollen stomachs and the dull eyes and poorly healing wounds characteristic of malnutrition—such children are not to be seen in such numbers.... Many poor people now have food"(Kotz 1979). These researchers were clear in their assessment that it was public policy—the expansion of food stamps, school lunch, and school breakfast that made the difference.

By the mid-1970s food stamps were a universal entitlement available to all citizens as long as they met the income requirements, regardless of whether they worked or not. As such, food stamps were the closest thing we have ever had to a universal floor under wages in the United States. The degree to which the public and policy makers across the political spectrum were galvanized to take action in the face of visible malnutrition speaks to the success of social movements in pushing the state to guarantee a basic level of economic security. The food safety net of the 1970s was explicitly intended to protect citizens against the worst ravages and hardships associated with poverty. However, expanding food assistance succeeded precisely because it remained a partial, supplemental solution. Even with food assistance, poor people still need to work to pay for shelter, clothing, and other necessities. More transformative demands like the NWRO's campaign for a guaranteed income failed precisely because they challenged the idea that poor people must go to work to meet their basic needs.

The expansion of the food stamp program in the 1970s was rooted in demands for care that were enacted through the welfare state. Social movements, advocates, and citizens offered a clear response to the question, "how should care happen in an inclusive democracy?" (Tronto 2013, 10). To be a citizen in a land of plenty meant to be able to have enough food to sustain oneself, and a broad range of Americans insisted that it was the role of the state to ensure that everyone had access to sufficient food. The modern food stamp program was a tremendous policy and public health achievement, virtually eliminating clinical malnutrition in the United States. But the program's success in eliminating severe hunger was quickly overshadowed by a political backlash against the War on Poverty and the gains of the civil rights movement more generally (Quadagno 1996, Neubuck and Cazenave 2001). The paradoxes of the growing food safety net in the twenty-first century are rooted in this backlash.

ORGANIZED ABANDONMENT

The tone of the debate around food assistance changed dramatically by the early 1980s. In the 1970s, social movements pushing to expand social and economic rights for poor people began to wane for a number of reasons, including direct infiltration and disruption of movements by the police and the FBI (Blackstock 1975). At the same time, economic elites in the US began to organize politically through new institutions like the Business Roundtable. Their goal was to "restructure state agencies that had been designed under the enormous emergency of the Great Depression (the New Deal) and its aftermath (loosely, the Great Society) to promote the general welfare" (Gilmore 2009), including welfare state programs like cash assistance to poor families, food stamps, Medicaid, and social security. By 1980, the ideas promoted by these business elites had gained national prominence in the figure of Ronald Reagan.

Reagan perfected the use of coded racial language meant to conjure an image of welfare users as Black—despite the fact that the majority of both welfare and food stamp recipients have always been white (Haney-Lopez 2014). He used thinly veiled racist terms like the welfare queen to build support for a political agenda aimed at dismantling and undermining state agencies that business leaders saw as problematic, including social protections for poor and working-class people. He defined care as the problem, asserting that the state was providing too much care to the poor at the expense of aggrieved tax payers (Edsall and Edsall 1992). Drawing on thinkers like Charles Murray, Reagan reframed welfare programs as harmful to poor people, arguing that assistance to the poor encouraged a culture of dependency (Murray 1984). He valorized work as the primary path to independence and voluntarism as the solution to poverty. By repeatedly portraying welfare dependents as living in luxury and contrasting them with economically struggling tax payers, Reagan successfully vilified welfare state programs among many white voters. He successfully pushed through cuts to welfare state spending in the early 1980s, including cuts to the food stamp program, in the midst of a deep recession (Poppendieck 2014, 263).

Alongside his attacks on welfare state programs, like food stamps, Reagan argued that the private sector and voluntary organizations were better equipped to address many of the nation's ills (Germani 1981). He popularized the idea that care should come from the local community, not the state. Efforts to reinvigorate the American tradition of voluntarism emerged alongside growing food insecurity due to welfare program cuts and a deep recession. People in struggling communities, hit by factory shut downs and cuts to social services, scrambled to respond to the rising needs of newly unemployed and insecure workers (Walley 2010, Pappas 1989). The efforts of faith-based organizations and community groups to respond to the early effects of deindustrialization gave rise to the modern food bank movement in the early 1980s and established the two-pronged approach to hunger we see today in the United States (Poppendieck 1998). Emergency food providers proliferated to fill in the gaps left by cuts to public programs like food stamps to meet the needs of hungry families.

One of the key welfare policy innovations Reagan championed was adding work requirements for public benefits like food stamps and cash assistance. Though some modest pilot welfare-to-work programs were put in place in the 1980s, these efforts were limited. The first meaningful work requirements for food stamps were instituted in 1996 as part of the federal welfare reforms passed under Bill Clinton's administration.

Clinton's campaign pledge to "end welfare as we know it" set him apart from other Democratic leaders. It signaled a willingness to abandon a Keynesian approach to the welfare state that would protect programs that redistribute resources to people when the market fails them. Instead, Clinton's ascendency marked the consolidation of a brand of market triumphalism, often referred to as neoliberalism, that saw free, unregulated markets as the solution to a whole range of social issues—including poverty and hunger (Maskovsky and Goode 2001). From a policy perspective, Clinton defined the solution to poverty as participating in the market as a worker, particularly for poor women with children who were the primary beneficiaries of cash and food assistance. Citizenship itself was redefined as both the right and the obligation to participate in markets.

Welfare reforms in the Clinton era directly undermined the gendered exemption from work for poor mothers caring for young children. Millions of poor women left the welfare rolls after the passage of welfare reform in the late 1990s, and when they did, they often lost their food stamp benefits. The diversionary tactics local welfare offices employed to discourage families from applying for cash assistance after the passage of welfare reform were also employed to discourage them from applying for food stamps (Davis 2002, Independent Budget Office 2008). Food stamp rolls plummeted after 1996, falling from twenty-five million in 1995 to just below seventeen million in 2000 (Wolkwitz 2007). The steep drop in the food stamp rolls set the stage for the revival of food assistance as a strategic policy intervention designed to meet the needs of the working poor.

SELECTIVE CARE

If the face of a starving child motivated the expansion of food stamps in the 1970s, it was the face of the working mom who could not afford healthy food that inspired the expansion of food assistance at the turn of the twenty-first century. In the wake of welfare reform, women entered the work force, but found they often could not move out of poverty, despite working full time

(Lein 2007, Newman 2001). The working poor emerged as a visible and sympathetic population, fulfilling their obligation to work but still struggling with incomes that kept them below the poverty line. The expansion of food assistance that began in 2001 under the George Bush administration was largely a response to the needs of poor mothers who could not make ends meet even though they were working. Changes to the food stamp program that made it easier for working families to access the program were part of a broader push to increase work supports, such as the earned income tax credit (EITC) for low-wage workers. Business leaders were largely supportive of increased wage subsidies because these programs made it easier for employers to keep wages low. Unlike the expansions of food assistance in the 1970s that were in many ways a response to social movements and their demands for wealth redistribution, the expansion of food assistance in the twenty-first century was essentially a give-away to low-wage employers. While many poor working families receive a boost to their income from SNAP and the EITC, those who do not fit the model of the working poor can be excluded from help.

During the George Bush administration, the expansion of federal food programs took place quietly. Reimagining food stamps as a work support was a technocratic response to long-term economic trends in the labor market that began in the 1980s. Throughout this period, manufacturing jobs, which provided stable work and middle-class wages for large numbers of working-class families, disappeared. These jobs were largely replaced by service-sector jobs that are lower paid and less secure. The kinds of jobs available to working-class households include care work of various kinds—cooking; looking after children, the ill, and the elderly; and house work.

change from.
in diet.

Broad changes in the labor market also had an enormous impact on the ways that Americans eat. Changes in the American diet over the past several decades have spurred concern over public health, obesity, and diet-related disease, which became central issues shaping food policy in the Obama era. The commodification of household labor has created a huge pool of cheap "help" that even low-income families can access. These cheap forms of help range from fast-food restaurants and processed, prepared foods in the grocery store to the proliferation of day-care centers and home health aides. These growing industries are the mainstay of employment growth in the United States, producing thousands of new, poorly paid jobs for the American working class. As Susan Thistle writes, "The conversion of women's domestic tasks into work done for pay has been the area of greatest job growth over the past thirty years" (Thistle 2006, 102). She argues that almost two-fifths of the increase in jobs since 1970 was due to market takeover of household and caring tasks. Some of the most remarkable growth has come in the food service industry, as Americans of all income levels increasingly eat food prepared outside the home. The factory-like production of fast food has been the key to lowering the costs of prepared food and putting it in reach of even poor households (Thistle 2006, Fantasia 1995, Schlosser 2002, Levenstein 1993). Even more rapid growth has taken place in the realm of routine domestic care for the sick, elderly, and young, and "the commercialization of women's domestic realm will continue to provide the bulk of new employment over the first decades of the twenty-first century" (Thistle 2006, 106).

As women moved into the labor force in large numbers, the commodification of domestic labor has produced a strained, stratified patchwork of market, familial, and state systems of care. But as Mona Harrington has argued, "We have come nowhere near replacing the hours or quality of care that the at-home women of previous generations provided for the country" (Harrington 2000, 17). As caring labor is increasingly commodified, we are confronted with the question, how much can we reorganize forms of care without imposing significant costs? As Sylvia Federici points out, "The degree to which the marketization of food production has contributed to the deterioration of our health (leading, for example, to the rise of obesity even among children) is instructive" (Federici 2012). Reliance on commodified forms of care for low-income households—fast food and prepackaged foods in particular—are increasingly understood as contributing to ill health and producing new forms of social instability.

Led by Michelle Obama's efforts, the Obama administration emphasized the role that programs like SNAP could play as both a work support and a public health intervention. However, in the face of the entwined crises of care, economic insecurity, and public health, the Obama administration's efforts to transform food programs were largely symbolic. For example, his administration changed the name of the food stamp program to the Supplemental Nutrition Assistance Program, or SNAP, to emphasize the nutritional impact of the program as part of the 2008 stimulus bill. This change was part of a broader push by Michelle Obama's Let's Move campaign to tackle rising rates of childhood obesity and diet-related disease. The emphasis on health and nutrition that defined the Obama administration's approach to food policy and was reflected in the passage of improved nutrition standards for school lunches and the program for Women, Infants and Children (WIC). But these narrow, targeted interventions failed to confront the power of a loosely regulated food industry to flood consumer markets with unhealthy foods. Nor did they do much to improve low-income households' purchasing power in ways that might enable them to afford healthier but more expensive food.

Obama-era concerns with health and well-being were grafted onto a food safety net that was structured first and foremost to encourage and support low-wage work, not to ensure a universal right to adequate, healthy food. President Obama's commitment to work-first welfare was in line with previous administrations, reflecting the staunch political consensus of welfare reform as a success. His approach to poverty and food insecurity was largely compatible with the organized interests of the business community that have dominated national politics since the 1980s. He attempted to give states greater flexibility in how they implemented work requirements for safety net programs in 2012. These efforts met a swift and furious backlash, with presidential candidate Mitt Romney running ads claiming that Obama was trying to "gut welfare reform." The Obama administration immediately backed off these minor changes, and Obama defended his record of helping to implement work requirements in Illinois as a state senator, signaling his strong commitment to work-first welfare despite his administration's vocal concerns with public health (Ball 2012).

THE POLITICS OF EXCLUSION

In the 1970s, profits began for fall for industrial manufacturing in the United States. Firms responded by pursuing a spatial fix, lowering labor costs by moving production to areas of the globe where labor was cheaper. Today, the growing sectors of the US economy have no spatial fix. Care of the elderly and sick, housekeeping, and the retailing of food and other consumer goods cannot be moved offshore. Since there is no spatial fix for these sectors, elites have pursued what Collins and Mayer have called a "relational fix," creating new categories of people within the working class who are more vulnerable to exploitation and who can be excluded from basic economic rights. Collins and Mayer argue that workfare and welfare reform were part of the creation of a race to the bottom in service jobs that tracked with the global race to the bottom in manufacturing (Collins and Mayer 2010). The institution of workfare, along with an undermining of immigrant labor rights and the creation of a large population of formerly incarcerated people who can be legally discriminated against in the labor market (Alexander 2010) exerts downward pressure on the wages and rights of all wage workers. This domestic race to the bottom has taken the form of both stagnating wages and salaries as well as increasingly informal labor arrangements—including many occupations in what is now called the "gig economy"—extremely short-term jobs, such as Uber drivers, with no formal relationship between employers and employees. The lives of the families in this book are intimately shaped by this race to the bottom. As I assisted people in applying for food stamps and accompanied them to welfare offices, packed bags with them in the food pantry, and shared meals with them in the soup kitchen, they shared their sense of slipping further behind. For many, the stable lives they yearned for felt increasingly out of reach.

Across the political spectrum, welfare reform continues to be heralded as a success precisely because TANF, the cash assistance program for poor families, continues to enroll far fewer people today than it did when reforms were passed. Success is never measured by how many people actually moved into work or escaped poverty, but how many are moved off of the rolls. The assumption is that if people are no longer receiving assistance, then they must be working. But the reality is that there are a growing number of Americans who are disconnected from both the labor market and state assistance. Six million people in the United States had no access to any income other than SNAP in 2010 (DeParle and Gebeloff 2010). The number of single mothers who are disconnected from both work and welfare has grown steadily since 1996 (Blank and Kovak 2008). Further, growing numbers of both men and women find themselves outside of or on the edge of the paid labor force and are struggling to find a way back in.

After a huge spike beginning in 2008, the unemployment rate slowly returned to pre-recession levels. In September 2018, unemployment stood at 3.7 percent, or 6.1 million people who wanted to work, but were not employed. However, the official unemployment rate only captures part of the story. The labor force participation rate—the percentage of US residents who are currently working—suggests a less rosy economic picture for American workers. The number of people who are actually working has remained far below pre-recession levels. Only 62 percent of all adults were employed in 2017—down from 66 percent in 2007. Labor force participation rates began to rise in the early 1970s as middle-class incomes stagnated. Women, including mothers of young children, began moving into the labor force in higher numbers. Labor force participation peaked at 67.3 percent of the adult population in 2000 and has been declining ever since. In the wake of the recession, labor force participation remains at a thirty-eight-year low. Men's participation in the labor market has steadily declined since 1950 (Bureau of Labor Statistics 2016). Low unemployment rates don't tell the full story because they don't count all the people who have given up on a labor market that has little demand for more workers.

Further, unemployment numbers tell us very little about the quality of the jobs people encounter when they enter the labor market. Employment numbers don't just count standard employees, with regular full-time jobs. This number includes anyone working, even if they only work a few hours a week and earn next to nothing as underemployed freelance or contract laborers. Freelance and contract workers grew from 10.1 percent of all workers in 2005 to 15.8 percent in 2015, and nearly 40 percent of people in these jobs have a bachelor's degree or higher. Within the part-time labor force, 6.4 million would have preferred full-time work (Katz and Krueger 2016). Even as the labor market has grown tighter, with record low unemployment rates, wages have stayed flat (O'Brien 2018).

There is a disconnect between an official economic recovery and the overwhelming sense of economic insecurity that is palpable among people at welfare offices and food pantries across the United States. This economic insecurity has become a driving force in US politics. Downward mobility runs the risk of creating a dangerous political instability. Just as the safety net has been drawn more tightly around the idea of work, workers like Nigel and the other families we will meet in this book are getting their legs kicked out from under them. Employers are abandoning their commitments to even basic tenets of the employer-employee relationship.

Work, as a system of distributing necessary resources to the bulk of the US population, has begun to fail in a range of ways. The commonsense belief that work is a way out of poverty is at odds with the reality that work has never been a particularly effective mechanism for distributing wealth, particularly for racialized populations living in the United States. For generations, African Americans and exploited immigrant laborers have been relegated to low or nonpaid, degrading forms of work that did not provide enough to sustain families with dignity and security. These insecure and exploitative labor conditions have become far more widespread in the twenty-first-century US economy. Many full-time workers no longer earn enough to afford basic necessities like food and shelter. The food safety net has been reconfigured to subsidize poor workers and exclude those who do not work, just as work itself has become more nebulous and less secure. The next chapter tells the stories of two families as they navigate the new terrain of a growing food safety net targeted to the working poor in an era where work itself is being redefined.

CHAPTER THREE

The Carrot and the Stick

Nydia, a thirty-five-year-old Puerto Rican woman with a bright smile and an infectious laugh, applied for food stamps at the local welfare office in North Brooklyn after the birth of her second child. She worked full-time and had planned on taking a full twelve weeks of unpaid maternity leave. Like many mothers, she cobbled together funds from her vacation, sick days, and savings to cover the expense of not working for three months. Her husband was "doing odds and ends," as she put it, working in construction. Together, it should have been enough to get them through twelve weeks without Nydia's paychecks. But a few weeks into her leave, her husband tore his rotator cuff and had to be in sling for a month. With both of them out of work, Nydia suddenly felt desperate. "I never felt the way I felt when I applied for food stamps. It was not a good feeling. I was like, holy moly, how am I going to feed my kids?" She considered cutting her maternity leave short and going back to work, but her mom convinced her to apply for food stamps instead so she could have more time at home with her son.

Nydia and her mother arrived at the local welfare office early in the day to make sure theirs wouldn't be a wasted trip. The lines at the welfare office often snaked down the block. It wasn't unusual to wait for several hours in the dingy waiting rooms before being told there were no appointments left for the day and to come back tomorrow. Nydia and her mother weren't taking any chances. They were there right as the office opened. After waiting for several hours, Nydia finally got in to see a caseworker, whom she described as "mean" and "talking down" to her.

Caught between the conflicting goals of restricting welfare for unemployed applicants and expanding food stamp use among the "working poor," front-line employees often see their job as policing the boundaries between those who genuinely deserve help and those who are trying to defraud the system. They rely heavily on official documents like tax forms and pay stubs to evaluate whether the applicant is eligible. Applicants face skepticism and suspicion as caseworkers try to make sense out of the extensive documentation that accompanies each application, which includes information documenting residence, income, expenses, assets, and citizenship status.

Lester Towns, a middle-aged African American man who works at the North Brooklyn welfare office processing food stamp applications felt that applicants "don't want to put income down." He continued: "They don't want to put their bank accounts down. They don't want to fill out anything that they feel that's gonna make them not receive food stamps." This was echoed by Tish Taylor, an African American woman who has worked in the welfare office for over twenty years. "We've been working here so long," she said, "we know how to pull it out, the stuff that gets them in trouble. We know certain things, so we question it."

Eligibility specialists probe clients about two main issues: household composition and income, which both determine whether a household qualifies for food stamp benefits and how much it will receive. Clear documentation of income, especially with pay stubs, is one of the easiest ways for workers to make sense of a client's case. Clients who have no work or unstable work, work off the books, or receive some other form of irregular income are subject to far more scrutiny and have to document their income with letters written by either an employer or the applicant. Taylor described her interactions with these clients: "We say, 'Bring the pay stubs,' and when the client says they don't get pay stubs, we get a letter, which we *know* is a fraudulent thing."

Nydia's caseworker quickly discovered that her husband and children were already in the computer system because they received health insurance benefits from the state. Nydia had health insurance through her job, but it wasn't very good and it was expensive to cover her children under this plan. She and her children's' father are not officially married, though they have lived together for fifteen years. Since he does not have a regular income, he and their two children qualify for public health benefits through the Medicaid program. This raised a red flag for the worker who began questioning why Nydia and her husband weren't officially married.

Nydia was put off by this line of questioning and responded, "That's none of your business. He's the father of my children." With tensions rising, the case worker pointed out that, "a lot of these cases are fraud." This accusation upset Nydia and she started crying right there in the food stamp office. "And then when I started crying, I felt humiliated. That's how I felt. And I was like, oh no. Heck no." She pulled herself together and told the caseworker, "I'm not here because I want to be. I'm here because I need help. You know, I need help to feed my children. I'm not asking for no cash assistance. I have a job and I plan on going back to work, but I need help. And you know what? I work. I pay taxes. I think I'm entitled to this. Whether it's for this little bit of time or for an extended period of time, I need this."

Nydia had said the magic words. She asserted her deservingness in clear terms, arguing that she was not asking for cash assistance, had a job, paid taxes, and was entitled to food assistance for her children. Instantly the tone changed. The case worker asked for Nydia's pay stubs and paperwork related to her maternity leave. As Nydia put it, the caseworker "brought it down and the rest of the process was smooth." Because she had clear documentation, including pay stubs, Nydia was able to make her employment legible, visible, and verifiable to the food stamp office. Her ability to produce paperwork that corroborated her identity as a working mother, someone who "has a job," eased the tensions in their interaction and convinced the case worker that she deserved assistance. Her application was processed that day and three days later she was able to go grocery shopping for her family. Once she returned to work at the end of her maternity leave, her family continued to receive food stamps because her income was low enough that they still qualified. Nydia had a clear understanding that it was not her status as a mother that entitled her to assistance, but her status as a worker. She understood the new terms of deservingness in part because it was her job to help other women access income supports.

Nydia worked as a family assistant at a day care center in North Brooklyn, where she helped connect the low-income families at her center with benefits and programs, from parenting classes to housing assistance. Nydia was an outspoken advocate for SNAP, in large part because she benefitted from the program herself. She used her own experience when talking to other parents about the food stamp program, particularly when they were embarrassed or hesitant to apply. "I try to encourage our parents to enroll. A lot of them are afraid ... and I keep telling them that it's not welfare. It's not the same thing. It's food assistance that they are entitled to, especially for their children. With the stigma with food stamps, they're embarrassed, and I'm like, you have no reason. I'm employed. I don't make excellent money, but I make pretty decent money and I don't have an issue [with getting SNAP] at all."

Since 2001, the fastest-growing demographic on the food stamp rolls has been low-wage workers and their families.[1] Many participants, like Nydia, work full-time in offices, day care centers, and restaurants and earn barely enough to put them over the poverty line. Like Nydia, over a third of food stamp recipients have at least some college. Nydia's insistence that food stamps "are not welfare," but food assistance that working families "are entitled to" echoes the language of political elites who have attempted to reduce the stigma of certain welfare state programs, particularly for women in the workforce who are struggling financially.

THE CARROT: SUBSIDIZING WORKING MOTHERS

Food stamps have seen a remarkable turn-around from a stigmatized welfare program in the 1990s to a valued "work support" today. A 2010 article in the *New York Times* declared that the program "once stigmatized, has found acceptance" (DeParle and Gebeloff 2010). The article argued that "after tough welfare laws chased millions of people from the cash rolls, many into low-wage jobs as fast-food workers, maids, and nursing aides, newly sympathetic officials saw food stamps as a way to help them" (DeParle and Gebeloff 2010). As legal scholar David Super demonstrates, "in the six years from 1996 to 2002, the Food Stamp Program shed its skin, transforming from a political pariah to the beneficiary of a multi-billion dollar benefit expansion proposed by George W. Bush (at the same time he was attacking a host of other means-tested programs)" (Super 2004). The efforts to ease access to food stamp benefits were largely motivated by a new attitude among administrators and policy makers that reframed food stamps as a "work support" for low-wage workers.

Attempts to destigmatize programs like food stamps stand in stark contrast to the rhetoric that surrounded welfare reform legislation passed in 1996. In the mid-1990's, politicians zeroed in on poor women deemed "dependent" and argued that these women must be pushed into a job—any job—no matter how low paid or insecure. But welfare reform's promise of self-sufficiency through employment proved somewhat illusory. Most women who left the welfare rolls found low-wage jobs, but very little relief from the grinding poverty they had known when they were receiving assistance. Welfare reforms were enacted in a period of declining job prospects and stagnating wages for many working and middle-class households. In this context, full-time working mothers, like Nydia, who struggled to make ends meet emerged as a new deserving poor and welfare spending and program administration were transformed to boost the value of these workers' low wages. The policy approach since 1996 has been to modify and expand some means-tested welfare benefits to "make work pay," especially for working mothers, by subsidizing low wages.

The largest contributing factor to the remarkable rise in the food stamp rolls between 2001 and 2012 has been a deteriorating economy that no longer works for many workers. Nydia is one of them. Food stamps have become increasingly important, not only for the very poor—families struggling to make ends meet at jobs paying the minimum wage or less—but for people attempting to maintain a toehold on the middle class. As college educations (and even advanced degrees) lose their value in an increasingly competitive job market, more and more families and individuals turn to welfare programs to retain some level of security. "Work supports" become the thin line that keeps them from slipping into situations of real hardship.

Nydia's family was typical in this regard. Nydia was born and raised in North Brooklyn. She and her two siblings grew up on a tree-lined block of cramped tenement buildings. Her dad worked as a mechanic for forty years in a plastic bag factory on the nearby waterfront. He walked to work every morning before he retired. When Nydia and her siblings were young, her mom worked part time as a nurse's aide and as a cashier. Nydia's family was by no means wealthy, but when her dad retired, he was making $48 an hour, had a good pension, and received social security. Work had offered her family a strong sense of financial stability and security.

Nydia began working at the day care shortly after her father passed away. Like her father, Nydia's life is structured by work and family. In some ways her life has not changed much since her childhood. She still lives in the cramped railroad apartment where she was born and which she inherited from her parents. Like her dad, her life is centered on her neighborhood. She walks to work every morning and returns home every night to care for her two children. Just like her dad, she is represented by a union at work and sees herself as part of the American working class.

Despite these similarities, what it meant to be working class in the New York of Nydia's youth and what it means today are dramatically different. Perhaps most dramatically, Nydia is the main breadwinner for her family. Her husband, with only a high school diploma, struggles to find steady work. Dramatic changes in the neighborhood, the city and the overall economy mean that families like hers struggle for a sense of stability and security. The nearby waterfront, once packed with large, industrial employers, where men like Nydia's dad came to expect jobs for life, is unrecognizable today. Old factory buildings have been demolished or transformed into luxury housing built for a wealthy elite. Income inequality has skyrocketed, undermining the middle class and transforming the experience of work—as well as the rewards associated with it.

Today, poor workers are encouraged to rely on both an insecure labor market and the welfare state to make ends meet. Nydia's job was, quite literally, to help families access the work supports they needed to make up for the insufficient wages and benefits they receive from their employers. Welfare state programs, including the earned income tax credit, subsidized child care, food stamps, and expansions of other tax credits have all grown in size and scope since the mid-1990s (Bitler et al. 2010, Moffitt 2015). In fact, overall spending on welfare programs for the poor has increased dramatically since the mid-1980s and most of this increased spending has gone into the pockets of poorly paid workers (Moffitt 2015). These carrots incentivize low-wage work for poor families and make it possible for them to survive in jobs that pay below subsistence wages or to weather unpaid gaps in employment because of the birth of a child or a family illness. The term *work supports*, often used to describe SNAP, purposefully emphasizes work as the basis of deservingness. Nydia was not seen as deserving simply because she had hungry children to feed. Instead, it was her status as a worker that shifted the tone of her interaction with the food stamp caseworker, garnering respect and help rather than skepticism and scorn in her attempt to access to federal food assistance.

Her interaction with her caseworker reflects a much broader shift in the expectations around motherhood, work, and welfare in the latter half of the twentieth century. In 1975, only 39 percent of women with children under the age of six worked. By 2000, 65 percent of all mothers with children under six were employed (Bureau of Labor Statistics 2010). Millions of women entered the paid labor force as the second-wave feminist movement in the 1960s and 1970s contested the idea that women should be dependent on men and the wages they earned. Highly visible white, middle-class feminists advocated for a feminism built in their own image—demanding entry into the workforce on equal footing with men. As bell hooks pointed out, white middle- and upper-class feminists, "were so blinded by their own experiences that they ignored the fact that a vast majority of women were (even at the time *The Feminine Mystique* was published) already working outside the home, working in jobs that neither liberated them from dependence on men nor made them economically self-sufficient" (hooks 1984, 96). Feminists of color contested this vision of women's emancipation, arguing for an explicitly antiracist, socialist feminism capable of addressing the oppression of poor women and women of color (Combahee River Collective 1977). Women of color who, historically, were more likely to work outside the home, understood that employment under capitalism was insufficient to guarantee freedom from poverty, racism, and sexual abuse for poor and working-class women (Taylor 2017).

Unfortunately, the vision of second-wave feminism prevailed in part because it was entirely compatible with the transformations in the broader political economy that were taking place in the same moment. Declining incomes and benefits for many men pushed women into the workforce. The commodification of many of the domestic tasks carried out by women in the home opened up new markets and avenues for profit making in an emerging service economy that was hungry for both women's labor and their consumer dollars in industries like fast food, childcare, and elder care. The achievements of middle- and upper-class women in the workforce—and the normalization that women could and should work—was weaponized against poor women in the welfare reform era.

Poor women who wanted to stay home with their children and care for them were painted as lazy and pathological—passing down the pathology of a poor work ethic to their children. The claims of welfare rights organizers in the late 1960's, that raising children was work that must be compensated by the state, were totally absent from the public debate over welfare that took place in the 1990's. Instead, pushing women into the workforce was framed as a panacea to a whole host of social ills, from poverty to children's school achievement to mental health. Welfare reforms pushed millions of poor women off the welfare rolls and into low-paid jobs that did little to advance their economic position, in what Meda Chesney-Lind has called "gender equality with a vengeance" (Chesney-Lind 1995).

Mothering has long been stratified in the United States, with some women being valued as mothers and others prevented from caring for their children as they would like (Mullings 1997,

Colen 1995). African American mothers in particular have long struggled for the right to care for their own children on their own terms. The emphasis on work-first welfare redefined good mothering, particularly for poor mothers, as working for wages to provide monetarily for children and, in so doing, provide them with a "good role model." Analysts from across the political spectrum found common ground on the need to enact policies that would support poor women as workers (Duncan and Chase-Lansdale 2002).

What has emerged is a kind of de-gendered welfare state that benefits low-wage employees and their children in ways that empower some mothers while undermining the ability of unemployed mothers to meet these new expectations around work and motherhood. The needs of mothers to care for their children are subordinated to the requirement that mothers participate in the formal labor market in order to access assistance from the state. In this regard, Nydia is one of the lucky ones. She has a steady, regular job. It might not be well paid, but it affords her easy access to a whole host of work supports that keep her family afloat in an uncertain economy. However, Nydia's access to work supports depends on her maintaining an identity as a worker or maintaining a connection to a worker. Women who can't establish an identity as a worker, even for a short time, have a very different experience when they seek assistance to feed their families.

THE STICK: PUNISHING "NON-WORKING" MOTHERS

Adwa's experience differed markedly from Nydia's precisely because her relationship to the formal labor market was more tenuous. Adwa and her sons were regular fixtures at the North

Brooklyn Pantry. She was a petite, Black woman in her mid-thirties who had immigrated to the United States from Gabon fifteen years earlier. Her sons, ages seven and nine, had a close relationship with one of the cooks at the soup kitchen. The two boys often sat on the stairs, working out math problems, as volunteers bustled around in the crowded kitchen below, chopping vegetables and stirring pots of pasta or boiled potatoes.

Adwa usually sat at one of the folding tables in the dining area, reading or chatting with the church pastor. She and I had not interacted much beyond brief hellos as I dished out whatever was on the menu to her and her sons until she came to see me during my regular hours for food stamp outreach at the North Brooklyn Pantry. Each week, volunteers put flyers in the pantry bags to let people know they could come by to get help filling out a SNAP application or get help if they had a problem with their food stamp cases. Adwa showed up on a rainy Monday afternoon, taking her time removing her wet coat and shaking the water off her bag before extracting a sheaf of papers from the welfare office neatly held together with a rubber band. She announced to me that she had a problem and she hoped I could help. The most recent notification she had received informed Adwa that her public assistance case was being moved from the welfare office near her house in Brooklyn to one far out in Queens. She had never been to that part of Queens before and she was not sure how to get there. She also had no idea why her case was being moved in the first place. She was agitated and wanted to know if I could figure out why they had moved her case and if it could be moved back. As we sat and talked, I quickly realized that this small, most likely erroneous, inconvenience was one of many Adwa had navigated with the welfare office over the past two years.

Unlike Nydia, Adwa did not have a job or paperwork that established her as worker when she first applied for assistance. This fundamental difference had a huge impact on Adwa's interactions with her caseworkers and with her family's experience of hunger. Adwa had applied for assistance two years before for herself and her two sons. Her husband had been in a car accident and was arrested for drunk driving and reckless endangerment. It was not his first offense. At the hospital, a social worker recommended that Adwa apply for public assistance because her husband had been the family breadwinner and his likely incarceration would leave Adwa and her sons with no income. At first, she was unsure, but the social worker explained the program and Adwa did not see any other immediate options for her family, so she enrolled. She quickly discovered, however, that cash assistance was not simply a form of benign help. As she described it, "Sometimes lies sound good. Lies are pretty. You take it. You don't know that they're lying to you."

Adwa was taken aback by what she saw as the rude, dismissive, and condescending attitude she encountered at the welfare office. She was informed that she would have to perform a workfare assignment in exchange for any assistance she and her two children received. Workfare programs, like New York City's Work Experience Program (WEP), were one of the primary innovations of welfare reform in the 1990s. Within two weeks of applying, Adwa was assigned to a workfare job in the parks department. She was expected to clean up the public parks for thirty-four hours a week in exchange for $535 in food stamps, $353 in cash, and a $400 housing allowance paid directly to her landlord each month, leaving her family well below the poverty line.

For mothers like Adwa, without employment in the formal labor market or friends and family who can help them, applying for assistance means giving up many of their basic rights as workers. Shortly after the Personal Responsibility and Work Opportunity Reconciliation Act passed in 1996, President Clinton's Labor Department ruled that workfare workers must receive minimum wage. This was a potentially radical decision because it would have created parity between workfare jobs and minimum-wage jobs in the private sector. It also would have undermined the long-standing relationship between welfare and work in the United States, a relationship in which welfare benefits for the poor are set low enough to "make any job at any wage a preferable alternative" (Piven and Cloward 1993, 36).

Food stamps were the key to undermining the radical potential of this decision. Shortly after welfare reform passed, the USDA approved simplified food stamp programs to bring food stamps in line with work-first welfare (Super 2004). Simplified programs allowed food stamp benefits to be counted as part of the minimum wage paid to workfare workers. The legally dubious practice of counting food stamps as wages had been in place since the creation of WEP in 1995 in New York City (Krinsky 2007). This federal policy decision brought New York City's practices in line with national legislation and provided legal cover for the city's welfare administration. By allowing food stamps to be counted as wages, the USDA's decision ensured that women enrolled in workfare programs would remain significantly worse off than women working in minimum-wage jobs in the private sector.

Being made to work in a job she did not choose for less than minimum wage was troubling to Adwa. Welfare recipients assigned to workfare programs were paid somewhere between $2.48 and $4.25 an hour in cash, depending on their family size. SNAP benefits made up much of the difference between these pitiful wage levels and the prevailing minimum wage, which was $7.25 per hour in New York State at the time of this research. Poor mothers like Adwa, who need assistance to care for their families in a moment of crisis, are paid in nonstandard currencies, creating stark distinctions between those with and without employment. In Adwa's case, she was earning $2.48 per hour in cash for her work in the city's parks. Unlike Nydia, who received food stamps with no strings attached and used her benefits to supplement her low wages once she returned to work, Adwa was made to work for every penny she received in food stamps.

In addition to the questionable practice of paying mothers in nonstandard currencies like SNAP benefits, welfare recipients in New York are offered very little choice about what kind of work assignment they are given. Adwa had hoped to be able to go to school and finish her associate's degree,[2] but at the time very few welfare recipients were allowed to count education as part of the cash assistance work requirements. As Adwa put it, "It's like they force you to do certain things that you don't want. You cannot even do the work you want. They impose you to work what they want. Whatever the schedule, bad or good, you have to do what they want you to do.... You have to work on Sunday. You have to work on Saturday. And if you don't work on Saturday, they fire you" Adwa found it particularly difficult to manage the demands of the welfare office with her parenting responsibilities. "They create a situation where you, the recipient, will have a problem with ACS (child protective services) because you will get the children late from an afterschool program or, you know, day care." At the heart of these challenges is a prevailing belief that the most important thing a mother can do for her children is provide them a good role model as a worker—no matter how low paid, inflexible or coercive that job might be.

By the time Adwa came to see me, she had been sanctioned off her family's case for missing a day of her workfare assignment. Women assigned to workfare have no sick days or leave. Being late or missing part of one's workfare assignment can result in a sanction that reduces the family's welfare benefits or cuts them from benefits entirely. Sanctions for failure to comply with the myriad of rules and regulations are extremely common in the cash welfare system, and they effect food stamp benefits. Twelve states currently employ full-family sanctions, meaning all family members, including children, lose food stamp benefits if the adult on the case fails to comply with work rules or any other requirements (United States Department of Agriculture 2017). In New York State, partial sanctions are applied to SNAP, cutting off only the adult's portion of food stamp benefits. Once she was sanctioned, Adwa's food budget for a family of three was cut to a budget for a family of two. At the time I met her, her children were getting $153 in cash assistance, $325 in food stamps, and $141 in rent assistance each month. Adwa was attending school on her own and cleaning other people's homes off the books for work.

Sanctions are intended to be the "sticks" that get welfare recipients to comply with work rules. Cutting the adult portion of the benefits was meant to motivate women like Adwa either to comply with her workfare assignment or, preferably, to find a job. In the words of Ron Haskins, one of the architects of welfare reform, "Mothers on welfare, even those with young children, should be encouraged, cajoled, and, when necessary, forced to work" (Haskins 2006).

Cutting food stamp benefits in order to force compliance with welfare rules or labor market participation is a particularly cruel punishment for women with children. Adwa was a thrifty and inventive cook. She cooked large meals that could last three days with lentils, rice and a bit of chicken and greens. Every time I visited her sparse apartment, a large pot simmered on her stove. But she had struggled to keep her family fed when they had a full food stamp budget for a family of three. Once she was sanctioned and their food stamp budget dropped from $526 a month to $325, feeding them all became even more difficult. Work requirements and the sanctions that are used to enforce them meant Adwa's family slipped deeper into poverty and food insecurity.

Like most people in her predicament, Adwa looked for work to support her family. She got a job as a cashier. She was making the minimum wage of $7.25 an hour, but her employer would only give her twenty hours a week. They scheduled her to work nights and weekends when her children were not in school and the pay did not even come close to covering her expenses. Adwa rejected the idea that good mothering meant holding down a job and providing a good role model for her children. She was not opposed to work, but she was frustrated by the inability of both the low-wage jobs that were available to her and the welfare office to accommodate what she saw as her crucial caretaking responsibilities.

Her role as a mother, with all the duties that entailed, came into direct conflict with the demands of both welfare and low-wage work. "The cashier job, they don't care." Adwa gestured to her children, sitting at the small table working on their homework in the sparsely furnished living room. "If I am at work and leave them, they will not do what they are doing. The manager will not care that I need to supervise the children. They don't care. What they need is, what they care about is that you provide the service they want from you."

Given the rigid schedules imposed on women by both the welfare office and low-wage employers, Adwa looked to the informal labor market as an alternative to bring in some cash and make up the difference between the aid she received for her sons and the needs of the household. Though this off-the-books work had more flexible hours, it was unstable and unreliable. Adwa sometimes took jobs just for one day. Others she might have for a few months. But with no formal employment relationship and no labor protections, these jobs were constantly in flux. Her most recent regular client had stopped using her the week before we met, putting Adwa back to square one with no regular or reliable income. She had been cleaning a man's Manhattan home and office for $15 an hour. "The guy says, 'Oh no, it's too much money.' And then he lopped down my salary, my days. Maybe he hires a Spanish [maid], paying her maybe $9 or $10 for all of this mess. That's not fair to me."

Food aid is used by the welfare agencies to coerce women like Adwa into accepting the role of a "good mother" who models good behavior for her children by going to work, earning wages, and submitting to the needs of her employer. The goal of welfare after the passage of welfare reform is to move women like Adwa into the labor force—to take any job at any wages. Sanctioning women who resist this idea of the "good mother" and cutting off their food stamp benefits purposefully creates hardship for these families to induce them into adopting the 'correct' behavior. It is reflected in the inordinate pressures put on women who enroll in cash welfare programs to become "job ready" at the same time that jobs in the United States are far from being "mother ready." Unlike Nydia, who had a partner at home with the flexibility to take care of her children, Adwa had no help. As an immigrant, she was separated from her extended family by an ocean, and her children's father was incarcerated. Like Nydia, she worried about how to feed her children. But unlike Nydia, turning to the welfare office did little to alleviate her stress.

The kinds of assistance available to Nydia, who could provide paperwork proving that she was employed, including a full food stamp allotment for her family, the earned income tax credit, unemployment insurance if she lost a job, and social security credits, were out of reach for Adwa. Flexible workers like Adwa, who work in temporary or short-term jobs, often find it difficult to establish their employment status in their interactions with welfare office workers and other state agencies. Working essentially as a day laborer, Adwa had no paystubs, no tax forms, no employer who could write a letter on her behalf, and no evidence beyond her word that she did, in fact, work. The unstable work that she found did not come close to providing enough money for her family to consistently afford basic necessities like rent and food and made her continued engagement with the welfare office necessary.

Though Adwa was sanctioned off her family's public assistance case, she still had to regularly report to the welfare office to provide documentation of her circumstances to keep her sons' benefits. These interactions with caseworkers were both disorienting and demoralizing. Though moving individuals "from welfare to work" was a mantra of welfare reform, the real emphasis for front-line employees in New York City has become moving people through the system as quickly as possible. Jose Nieves, a middle-aged Latino man who has worked as a caseworker for over a decade, described his job as "doing quantity, not quality." Antoinette Walker, an older African American woman who works in the same office, agreed. "You're pushing them through. You just get enough information to process and then keep them moving." Adwa described her interactions as hostile. "[They ask] Where is your pay tab? Where's your this? What are you doing with the time? What are you? What is this? What is this? You don't ... they make you lost. They trap you with all kinds of questions. Sometimes I can't even respond properly." Unlike Nydia, Adwa did not have a way to establish herself and her children as deserving in the eyes of the caseworkers with whom she interacted. The skepticism, brusque attitudes, and dismissiveness she encountered at the welfare office was unwavering.

WALKING AWAY FROM WELFARE *help*

When Adwa first came to see me about her case being moved to an unfamiliar welfare office, I did what I had often done, I emailed someone at the welfare office to see if they could fix the problem. I was part of a network of SNAP advocates at food pantries and soup kitchens across New York City who had been trained by the Food Bank for New York City to advocate on behalf of food stamp recipients when problems arose with their cases. The city council had been pressuring New York City's Human Resources Administration to do something about the long lines outside neighborhood welfare offices, where people often waited for hours before they could even get in the door. I had sent dozens of these emails for pantry clients for both large and small issues related to their SNAP benefits. But Adwa's case was different because she had a cash assistance case. Though it was clear that her case had been moved due to an administrative error, caseworkers steadfastly refused to respond to the issue over email. Just as working mothers could more easily access

adv a cog

food stamp benefits, they could also more easily access help when problems arose with their cases.

Adwa and I had to handle her issue the old fashioned (and far more time-consuming) way, going in person to the welfare office to see if we could get someone to fix the problem. We made two trips to the welfare office to try and remedy the original issue of her case being moved arbitrarily to a new welfare office. Each of these visits took the better part of a full day, sitting on worn plastic chairs in overcrowded waiting rooms. With no indication of how long it would be until we were called back to talk to a caseworker, we alternated between silence, idle chit chat about our children, and eavesdropping on the conversations going on around us.

Because everyone is there for the same reason, conversations often turn to complaints about the welfare system and advice about how to best deal with any number of problems that might arise. On our first attempt at rectifying the situation, we sat near a middle-aged woman in dark jeans and a sweatshirt with grey streaks in her hair. She was commiserating loudly with the thin woman seated next to her about her frustrations with cash assistance. Like Adwa, she had been cut from her case for failure to comply with a work assignment. She had missed a day working in the subway because her child had been sick. She had been to the office three times to try and clear up the matter with her caseworker, to no avail. The woman complained that the cash she received from the welfare office was hardly worth the work she was required to do. However, losing the full food stamp allotment was devastating. Talking about how she needed the full food stamp allotment to feed her family, she declared "forget the cash. Just give me the Medicaid and the food stamps." Several of the people sitting nearby murmured in agreement.

Adwa listened intently to the woman's complaints. Her eyes narrowed as she considered the possibility of walking away from cash assistance. She turned to me and wondered aloud, "maybe it is better to have only the food stamps. Maybe they would leave us in peace." Her children only received $294 in cash and rent assistance. If she were added back onto her family's food stamp case, their benefits would increase by $201, nearly making up for the loss in cash and rent assistance. Adwa had recently rented out a room in her two-bedroom apartment. She and her children slept in the second bedroom. Her new roommate covered nearly all of the rent for her rent-controlled apartment, so the rent assistance was less important now. It might be worth it, she mused, if it meant she would no longer have to deal with the humiliation of constantly reporting to the welfare office.

Many families voted with their feet, closing cash assistance cases and instead choosing to receive just food stamps and Medicaid. As Soss, Fording, and Schram demonstrate, this "self-sanctioning" is more likely among whites because "labor markets and social networks are more likely to provide income alternatives for low-skilled whites than for low-skilled Blacks" (Soss, Fording, and Schram 2011, 165). Jose Nieves, a welfare office worker who certifies cash assistance cases reported that "a lot of people don't even care about the money because there is no money." He reported that clients often ask him, "Is there any way I could get food stamps and Medicaid? You know, they'll get a job off the books because it's humiliating; you're getting in my business. And if you have children, health care is a priority. They don't want this chump change. It's a matter of survival. They need this Medicaid. They need this food stamps. They don't want to be here."

However, walking away from welfare was a risk Adwa felt unable to take. After months of navigating an unresponsive,

illogical
punitive
natural

punitive, and error-prone welfare system to maintain the meager benefits her children received, Adwa was afraid that giving
up her children's cash assistance case and trying to reopen a new
food stamp case could very well throw her family into even
deeper hardship. The sanction that cut her off from her family's
food stamp case was a durational sanction, meaning she was
barred from getting any food stamp benefits for six months as a
punishment for failing to comply with her workfare assignment.
It was unclear if this sanction would still apply to her if she
closed her cash case and tried to reopen just a food stamp case
instead. It seemed likely that she could end up in a situation
where her family still only received the food stamp allotment
for a family of two and they would no longer have any cash or
rent assistance for six months until the sanction was lifted. We
talked through the idea as we sat in the waiting room. Eventually Adwa sighed and dismissed the possibility. "You already
have a problem and they add to the problem."

In part, Adwa rejected the idea because trying to get a clear
answer for this question from a caseworker seemed daunting,
given her previous interactions. As ethnographers studying
welfare reform have shown, welfare office workers working in
understaffed, underfunded agencies are tasked with moving clients to "self-sufficiency" without adequate resources to do so,
given the circumstances of many clients lives and the labor market conditions they face (Morgen 2001, Kingfisher 1996, Watkins-Hayes 2009). The pressures on welfare workers produced a
style of interaction with clients that emphasized getting "enough
information to process and then keep them moving." In practice,
this meant case workers often conducted meetings with clients
as interrogations, asking for specific information and entering it
into their computers as quickly as possible without explaining

what was happening or why. When clients tried to ask questions or asked for clarification case workers often responded with obvious annoyance or with curt answers in bureaucratic jargon that made little sense to clients. If clients persisted in asking questions or expressed frustration or anger at the incomprehensible responses they received, caseworkers could, and often did, threaten to have security come and escort them out of the building.[3] Adwa, like many clients, had learned that caseworkers "tell you with their tone that they won't listen. So you just have to sit there."

Sanction policies, which are more punitive in states like New York that have large African American populations, are designed to teach poor women lessons that will transform them into "compliant and competent worker-citizens" (Soss, Fording, and Schram 2011, 9) and, ostensibly, move them into a jobs that can sustain them and their families. But Adwa was under no illusions about the kinds of work available to her and the limitations of a job as a solution to poverty. Her status as an immigrant, a single mother, and a Black woman made it more difficult for her to find regular work that could sustain her family and allow her to care for her children as she saw fit. She lacked social connections to help her find decent work. She faced discrimination in a labor market where immigrant women without an education routinely deal with low pay and exploitative conditions. And she had no family nearby to help shoulder the labor of caring for her children. As she put it, "'I'm the only person to support these two boys. My husband left. I don't look for charity, but my circumstances put me in this situation." As an informal worker in the gray economy, she fell outside the protections and wage subsidies provided to low-wage workers like Nydia. And because she failed to comply with the strict rules that govern workfare assignments, her family's food stamp budget was cut, creating additional hardships for her. She felt trapped by a welfare system that promised help but so often seemed to add to her troubles.

The workfare rules that govern cash assistance currently apply to some food-stamp-only cases as well. Adults between the ages of eighteen and forty-nine are required to perform a workfare assignment unless they are disabled or caring for a child under the age of eighteen. House Republicans have introduced legislation in the new Farm Bill that would expand work requirements for food stamp recipients to all adults unless they are caring for a child under the age of six. Under these proposed rules, many mothers like Adwa would be forced to show they are working or be cut off even from food assistance. In 2016 the USDA estimated that there were 3.5 million households with children who had no official income other than SNAP (Cunnyngham 2018). An earlier study found that these families survived by living with family and friends, often in exchange for food or housework, doing odd jobs and day labor, and skipping meals (Wilson and Estes 2014). It is likely that many families whose only income is SNAP have either walked away from cash assistance, are barred by TANF time limits and other restrictions, or never bothered to apply for cash assistance because they don't know about the program or have heard that help is not worth the hassle (Edin and Shaefer 2016). The proposed rules to expand SNAP workfare requirements to families with children would have devastating effects on these families and mothers like Adwa, who have no pay stubs, no paperwork, and no regular employer who can write a letter on their behalf showing that they do, in fact, work.

The road for Adwa to receive food assistance for her family was filled with far more barriers, disruptions, and risks than for

Nydia because she lacked a verifiable identity as a worker. Adwa was many things, including a mother, a student, and a day laborer, but none of these identities qualified her for the kind of work supports that comprise the welfare state in the United States. Though she desperately needed support, she faced challenges accessing food stamps, unemployment insurance, social security, or the earned income tax credit, given the kinds of work that were available to her and her need for flexibility to care for her children. Food stamps, which provided a significant boost to Nydia's income, came with significant burdens for Adwa's household, even though Adwa was in greater need.

THE CHANGING FACE OF WORK AND FAMILY

Lawrence Mead's 1992 book *The New Politics of Poverty: The Nonworking Poor in America* provided much of the ideological rationale for workfare programs implemented as a part of welfare reform. In the book, he argues that the welfare state fails "not because it does too much or too little for the poor, but because it did not set behavioral standards for the dependent." He singles out the non-working poor, asking "whether these parents, both fathers and mothers, could work more than they do, and why they do not." These questions, he asserts, "are the leading questions in social policy today." By the mid-1990s the political consensus around this question was unequivocally that these non-working parents could and should work more and that public policy must be transformed to push, cajole, and enforce compliance with work norms.

The push toward work, however, was firmly ensconced in the rhetoric of family values. Work was not valued simply as a path to economic independence. Work was laden with moral values and reconstructed around the idea of parental responsibility. Care, for poor mothers, was redefined as the responsibility to provide financially for their children. Poor working mothers who held down jobs but struggled to make ends meet became sympathetic, moral subjects because they exposed the contradictions at the heart of welfare reform.

Welfare reforms were justified through the claim that work was the best, perhaps the only, solution to poverty. The mantra that "a job is your path out of poverty" was repeated over and over in the push for welfare reform. Poverty was not, in the view of centrist Democrats like Bill Clinton, the result of exploitative employers who refused to pay living wages or the failure of the safety net to provide economic security. Poverty was caused by the refusal or the failure to hold down a job. Women moved off of the welfare rolls by the millions and went to work in the burgeoning service economy; however, despite upholding their end of the bargain, they did not find themselves lifted out of poverty (Lein 2007). Instead they found themselves still having to make hard choices about whether to pay the electricity bill or buy food.

The expansion of food stamps and other work supports, like the earned income tax credit, was an attempt by policy makers to "make work pay" and a partial acknowledgment that work, by itself, is not actually a path out of poverty for poor families. What is missed, however, in the expansion of work supports, is the politics of how work is defined. As work has become more informal, flexible, and insecure, many forms of work have become illegible to welfare caseworkers who are tasked with sorting the working from the non-working poor. Caseworkers are under scrutiny from their supervisors, who, in turn, are under scrutiny from policy makers constantly on the lookout for "fraud, waste, and abuse" within the food stamp program. Supervisors look over each SNAP approval to ensure that undeserving or fraudulent applicants do not receive assistance. As a result, caseworkers feel pressure to establish a clear paper trail that proves how much a person earns, what their expenses are, and whether or not they meet the work requirements for SNAP. Applicants typically experience caseworkers as rude and disrespectful; however, much of this attitude comes from the pressures on caseworkers to maintain "quality control."

But not having a paper trail that demonstrates employment is not the same thing as not working. Lawrence Mead's question, whether the non-working poor could work more than they do, assumes a very narrow definition of work as employment in the formal labor market. Poor workers engage in all kinds of hustles to make ends meet, from cleaning houses as a day laborer and braiding hair to selling loose cigarettes and bootleg CDs. As Lester Spence points out, in order to survive, urban dwellers engage in unceasing labor that spans both the formal and informal economies (Spence 2015). Even before welfare reform, most women who received benefits from AFDC combined them with some kind of informal or off-the-books employment (Lein and Edin 1997). Women like Adwa still engage in informal work in order to pay the bills, but today these women are actively pushed off of state assistance, including food assistance in many states, unless they comply with the harsh demands of workfare.

Feminist political theorist Kathi Weeks argues that making people capable of working (through school, drug treatment, medical intervention, all kinds of rehabilitation, including prisons) "is a key function of the state. It is not the police or threat of violence that force us to work, but rather a social system that ensures that working is the only way that most of us can meet our basic needs. Working is what is supposed to transform subjects into the independent individuals of the liberal imaginary, and for that reason, is treated as a basic obligation of citizenship" (Weeks 2011, 7). Work is not defined as an activity or an exertion of effort, but as an employment relationship. As Raymond Williams notes, it is only in this sense that a woman actively caring for children and a home "can be distinguished from a woman who works" (Williams 1976). Adwa performs paid labor, cleaning other people's houses for cash off the books, but her relationship to any particular employer is uncertain, temporary, and extraordinarily flexible. She operates in a gray zone of employment that benefits the people who hire her but puts her at a disadvantage when she attempts to access assistance from the state. She is seen as suspect; her claims are subject to intense scrutiny and her deservingness is called into question over and over again. Her lack of attachment to an employer makes her an unsympathetic subject. Women like Adwa, who resist the idea that good mothering means being a good worker, are punished with a reduction in food aid and are forced to make up the difference through intensifying their labor or turning to charity.

In his history of the US welfare state, Michael Katz shows how "only those Americans with real jobs are real citizens, and this association has tightened considerably in the last few decades" (Katz 2001, 348). What has also tightened considerably is the link between work and access to public benefits that target the poor. Jane Collins and Victoria Mayer demonstrate that "those who even temporarily lose their footing within the labor market lose aspects of their citizenship" (2010, 16). Increasingly, one of those lost aspects is an entitlement to welfare benefits, including work supports for the working poor. Welfare benefits, retooled as work subsidies, have become a sorting mechanism—

both sorting the deserving from the undeserving poor and sorting the work that is rewarded from the work that remains unrecognized, unremunerated, and unsubsidized.

Non-working mothers can be punished, while working mothers are helped. Within the bureaucratic workings of the city welfare administration, New Yorkers without access to wages are part of the "categories of poor who are deemed appropriate to neglect" (Gupta 2012, 63). They are made into a social identity that is frowned upon, sweeping the streets and cleaning the parks and subways. "The suffering body must be recognized as morally legitimate, a qualification that turns out to be both exceptional and deeply contextual" (Ticktin 2006, 4). In the context of growing precarity, the transformed welfare state recognizes the suffering bodies that work for wages but cannot afford basic necessities like food. These low-wage workers are protected by rights and by a responsive welfare administration. The suffering bodies that do not have formal work and cannot afford adequate food, however, are not morally legitimate and hence unworthy of support. These distinctions were not lost on poor New Yorkers. I met many unemployed workers, like Nigel, who wanted not just work but "something on paper" that would afford them access to the myriad work supports available to low-wage workers.

Transforming the welfare state to subsidize low-wage labor may have broad popular and bipartisan appeal in the United States, but it represents a troubling shift in the reconfigured relationship between citizens, employers, and the state and, in turn, for parents and their children. Under this conservative, paternalistic, post-Fordist welfare regime, socioeconomic rights are tied to an obligation to work. In the absence of full employment, this policy approach inevitably intensifies inequalities among fractions of the working class. This post-Fordist welfare regime is an example of what Gavin Smith (2011) calls "selective hegemony," characterized by the extension of welfare protections to a select group to shore up hegemonic power. At the same time, other groups are excluded from the hegemonic project. Un- and underemployed workers surviving on the margins of a formal labor market confront an unresponsive, punitive welfare system. In reconstructing food stamps as a program that both subsidizes low wages and punishes unemployment, the growth of the food stamp rolls actually reinforces large-scale economic changes, including the expansion of low-wage labor markets and the maintenance of a stigmatized, marginal reserve army of labor.

Remaking programs targeted to the poor as work supports means motherhood is no longer protected as a form of necessary caring labor. These policy changes hurt mothers like Adwa who struggle to balance the demands of low-waged work and caring for their children under the constant threat of losing access to the meager forms of assistance available to them. At the same time, poorly paid workers like Nydia turn to work supports from the state to make ends meet and maintain some level of continuity and stability for their families. Though their lives are not all that different, their circumstances and their experiences of food insecurity diverge because of policy decisions that value "real jobs" in the formal labor market and devalue the caring labor that both of these women do, raising children and keeping them fed.

Men are also caught up in the turn toward work support and, as we will see in the next chapter, this policy shift has profound effects on whether and how they are able to care for their families as well.

CHAPTER FOUR

Men, Food Assistance, and Caring Labor

When I first met Jimmy McWilliams, a forty-seven-year-old white man, he was living in temporary housing in a rundown building that housed two hundred men. He was enrolled in a drug treatment program after falling off the wagon a few weeks earlier. Jimmy had been sober for six years, but a series of cascading crises—the kind that often effect poor households—had pushed him over the edge.

Jimmy grew up in a working-class household in the Mott Haven neighborhood in the Bronx. His dad worked for the Metropolitan Transit Authority and his mom worked in nursing homes. Jimmy's family was one of the few white families who stayed as white flight and illegal blockbusting transformed the neighborhood from predominantly Irish in the 1940s to primarily Black and Puerto Rican by the late 1960s. Discriminatory urban renewal programs in the 1960s dramatically transformed the South Bronx. Hundreds of buildings were torn down to make way for highways that cut through formerly stable neighborhoods. Thousands of people were displaced, and homes, businesses, and jobs were destroyed (Caro 1974). Inside Jimmy's childhood home, his parents weren't necessarily the most loving, but they were able to provide for their family. As he put it, "One [parent] was a workaholic, the other was an alcoholic. But there was always a meal on the table no matter what time. If you came late, they kept it in the oven.... I guess the times were easier back then. My father worked for the transit, and my mother was a nurse, so they were making good money. Not great money."

Jimmy finished high school, but barely. He was not a good student, but he liked to work. He started doing odd jobs when he was nine or ten. In the summer, he sold newspapers to the local stores in Rockaway Beach, where his family had a summer house. In the winter, he made money shoveling snow. He had a lot of little hustles like that growing up. One of them was selling drugs. "I sold drugs for almost fifteen years; I only got caught three times. Best money I ever made." But after three arrests and a year in prison, he quit.

When he got out, he vowed to clean up his act. He found work at a unionized moving company, earning nearly $14 an hour in the 1990s. It was enough for him to live on. He had his own apartment and fit the image of the independent, self-sufficient worker. Jimmy liked working as a mover and he was good at it. He liked seeing how other people lived. He would have been happy to stay at that job, but after eight years of steady work, the company downsized and let him go.

His next job was working as a ticket taker and security guard with the Circle Line, a tour boat that circles Manhattan. He worked there for seven years—from 2001 until 2008. The pay was not nearly as good. He was hired at $9.25 and by the time his boss let him go in 2008 his pay had only risen to $9.27. Despite the poor compensation, he liked the work. He met interesting people from all over the world. He liked to joke with them and learn a little bit about their lives.

He met and married his wife during this period. She had an infant son when they met and Jimmy raised him like he was his own. They lived together in a small apartment in Brooklyn and Jimmy supported them with what he earned working on the boat and the small stipend his wife received from social security disability because their son has special needs. Their life had not been easy, but it was stable. Losing the job on the Circle Line turned out to be catastrophic and sent his whole family into a tailspin. The US economy was in the biggest slump since the Great Depression. Millions of Americans had lost their jobs and were frantically looking for work. The unemployment rate in New York City was climbing. Unsurprisingly, Jimmy had trouble finding work because he had a felony on his record. It wasn't long before they lost their apartment and ended up in a shelter. Jimmy was devastated. He hated living in the shelter and tried to find a way to get them back on their feet.

Eventually he found a job at a grocery store, helping to break up boxes a few days a week from noon to five o'clock for $60 a day off the books. It was something, so he took the job. But it wasn't enough to support himself, much less his family. After a few months, his boss offered him more hours. But there was a catch. "He asked me to come every day, six days a week and gave me from ten o'clock to five o'clock, but then he lowered the money down to $50 a day." Jimmy would be earning just below minimum wage with this arrangement. The frustration of having to accept such low pay grated on him. "So, then I was like I'm not doing this no more. I'm tired of taking all this bullshit with the boss. And I just quit." He wanted to work, but he also wanted to get paid for that work. "I gave up the job. Figured yeah, I'm smarter than this. I could find something better. I couldn't find nothing."

Depression set in when he turned up empty handed in his job search. It was 2009 and there were double-digit unemployment rates in the city. Jimmy stopped going to his Alcoholics Anonymous meetings. On his forty-seventh birthday, he decided to have a couple of sips of whiskey. "My wife said I knocked off a half gallon in ninety-two minutes. I went into straight blackout." The next thing he remembered was waking up at the police station. He had threatened his wife, punched a hole in the wall and started fighting with a neighbor. When he went back a few days later, she wouldn't let him in. She left his clothes in the downstairs hallway and he went into an in-patient substance abuse program. But after three days, they told him he had to leave. They did not take the Medicaid HMO he was enrolled in. He called his wife again. "I told her I wanted to come home. She said no. She seemed real depressed. It was raining, it was cloudy, it was cold. I took a bag of clothes with me and tried to swan dive off the Brooklyn Bridge." The police found Jimmy on the bridge. They talked him down and took him to the psychiatric ward at Bellevue, a public hospital. He stayed there for three weeks before he was transferred to transitional housing in North Brooklyn.

All of the tenants at the transitional housing facility had to be enrolled in public assistance in order for them to receive the $215 rent allowance and Medicaid. The owner of the facility was far less concerned with the rent subsidy than with each tenant's' Medicaid enrollment.[1] Residents were required to attend drug treatment meetings every day, whether they had a drug problem or not. It was an open secret among the residents that the landlord made money primarily off of the drug treatment services he provided. Several of the residents who lived there did not have drug problems, but simply needed a place to live. Others had active addictions and no interest in recovery. There was essentially no screening process to determine whether or not residents needed or wanted counseling. What most residents needed and wanted was housing. But since the housing allowance didn't pay for much, requiring drug treatment for all residents made the housing profitable. Residents were required to attend a minimum of four meetings a week, costing Medicaid $75 for each person in attendance.

Though his housing was a cash cow for the slumlord who owned his building, Jimmy was barely surviving. He was actively working on staying sober and thought the treatment program he was required to attend was a joke. He was living on $144 in cash assistance and $190 in food stamps each month. Public assistance also paid $215 in rent assistance to his landlord, the maximum rent allowance for a single person.

Jimmy came to the food pantry each week to pick up a bag of groceries and to have a hot meal the one night of the week that we served dinner. He often helped out, breaking down boxes for a few hours each week when he came to pick up a bag of food. Unlike most other public assistance recipients, Jimmy did not have to perform a workfare assignment in exchange for his benefits. He had an exemption for mental illness as a result of his suicide attempt, but he said he would have refused to do it because he saw workfare as a bad deal, both personally and for working people in general. "I can't see myself doing that. Because, say you work in the parks. Now, the average park worker gets about $8.50 an hour times 8, which is about $72 (a day) give or take. Now, for that week I'll be working down there for twenty-eight hours. So, for twenty-eight hours, I'm going to make the $72 he's going to make in a day. And that same twenty-eight hours, they want you working all week. It's like five hours a day, six hours a day." Jimmy's feelings about workfare reflected his analysis of the labor market as a whole. In his experience, employers were offering their employees less and expecting more from them. The falling price of his labor and the challenges of finding work over the course of his adult working life were driving factors in his recent breakdown.

Jimmy had been looking for work since he was released from the hospital. Unable to afford a Metro card for the subway, he often walked several hours each day going to warehouses and asking if they had anything available. "It's hard because once you get out—I walked over to Long Island City the other day, I had to walk all the way over the Greenpoint Bridge and about ten miles that way and about five miles that way. And it started getting too cold, and I started getting hungry. You go half way out, you don't want to go too far because you're only going to walk it back. It's not like you're going to search the places you want to search. Just to find out no, we're not hiring. Sorry. We're laying people off."

A few months after we met, he was offered a moving job paying $8 an hour, doing the same work he had done for nearly twice that amount twenty years ago. While Jimmy was relieved to find work, he was acutely aware of the falling price of his labor. "If I worked with this $8 an hour, I'll be making about $50 or $60 a day. I used to make $125 a day doing the same thing. I'm taking a $75 loss. But times are tough now." Over the course of his working life, Jimmy had seen his wages consistently going down from one job to the next. He reminisced about going to the grocery store as a younger man and "racking up," buying as much food as he could eat. But that seemed like an unrecoverable past. "I don't see it happening. I don't see none of that coming back. I don't even see the stability of living coming back anymore because it's always worse."

It would be easy to argue that Jimmy's troubles were largely due to his own mistakes—giving up a job at the grocery store that, perhaps, could have turned into something more sustainable, going after the easy money drugs offered instead of working hard in school as a young man, failing to control his addiction. What is undeniable, however, is that these kinds of mistakes are far more costly today than they were for Jimmy's father. Jimmy had grown up in a family with an alcoholic father *and* with dinner on the table every night. His father had the security of a union job that was stable, even when he was not. His father could go to work, do what was required of him, and receive a steady paycheck for his efforts.

Jimmy came of age in a radically different labor market. As Jimmy entered adulthood, industrial employment was on the wane and workers were expected to adapt to new conditions of competition and flexibility. Being willing and able is no longer enough to secure work for men like Jimmy who have only a high school education. As Wendy Brown argues, in this new context, people have been recast as "human capital who must constantly tend to their own present and future value" by acquiring new skills and education (Brown 2015). This was Jimmy's failure. He was not lazy or disinterested in work. However, his idea of work—as exertion that should be remunerated—was out of step with the reality of a highly differentiated labor force that thrives on self-improvement, competition, and flexibility.

The idea that work is and ought to be the primary path to independence is a hegemonic idea in American politics, and one which public policy actively enforces. Judith Shklar writes, "The opportunity to work and be paid an earned reward for one's labor" is the main source by which individuals gain public standing (Shklar 1998, 64). The reigning common sense in the United States is that earning makes one economically independent and, therefore, a citizen in good standing. Across party lines, work is seen as the panacea to nearly every social ill, from poverty to mental health to family stability. However, the going rate for many people's labor has fallen remarkably, a fact Jimmy understood intimately. He shared the belief that work could and should solve the challenges he faced. But his experience with employment taught him that he could no longer count on work as a solution to his family's economic distress. He saw no realistic alternatives. It was the sense that the good times were never coming back that drove Jimmy's depression and helped fuel the cascading crises he and his family experienced.

The idea that independence is the ability to sell one's labor for wages has its roots in America's racialized history. White males in the early American period contrasted their 'free labor' with that of enslaved people who worked but did not earn and aristocrats who did not work at all. "Ownership of one's labor and the ability to freely sell it, rather than ownership of productive property, became the basis for claiming independence" (Glenn 2002, 92). However, as Gordon and Fraser note, the idea that citizens can achieve independence and self-sufficiency through wage labor obscures the dependence of the worker on the employer. Workers like Jimmy are deeply dependent on their employers for wages.

In a capitalist economy, the employer/employee relationship shapes all other relationships, including relations between spouses, children, parents, extended families, and the fictive kin relationships people develop with close friends. Jimmy struggled to maintain his role as a provider, but as his value in the labor market fell, his role as an independent, wage-earning male was coming apart at the seams. In place of wages, Jimmy turned to public benefits to maintain kinship ties to his son.

The welfare state was built around the image of the wage-earning male. Benefits were designed to protect men when they fell out of the labor market because of job loss, disability, old age, or injury and to women with children when they lost a male provider. As James Ferguson points out, "The list of those requiring 'social' intervention (the elderly, the infirm, the child, the disabled, the dependent reproductive woman) traces a kind of photographic negative of the figure of the wage-earning man" (Ferguson 2015, 233).

Ownership of one's own labor established white men, in particular, as independent, deserving citizens. The loss of well-paid manufacturing jobs has been described as a crisis of masculinity that has largely been understood in terms of identity and employment (Bourgois 1996), but it is also experienced as a failure to care for family members or maintain kinship obligations (Edin and Nelson 2013). Gendered perceptions of welfare state programs targeted to the poor and the focus on single parent households headed by women have obscured our understanding of how men use welfare to participate in households where they may or may not reside to maintain family ties.

FATHERING THROUGH FOOD ASSISTANCE

Though he was not living with his son when I met him, Jimmy was committed to his role as a father. He struggled with severe hunger. He came to the food pantry and the soup kitchen every week to get a bag of food and a hot meal. Jimmy often went hungry and even sold his ulcer medication in order to get cash to buy food. Though he was categorized as a single person, he used a large portion of his food stamps every month to buy food for his son. Food stamps are not enough to feed a family or an individual for a month. Most recipients run out of food stamps after two weeks (Castner and Henke 2011). By contributing to his son's needs, Jimmy had even less.

"If I get them today, they're gone by Thursday easy. Real easy. I get $190. That would leave me with about $50.00 a week. It's about $7.00 a day to eat. And I'm trying to help her and the kid; forget it. He's got to have his snacks at school. He's got to bring a snack to school now. They don't give you snacks in school. He likes the little Oreos. And like five boxes is $20. Pop tarts when he comes home, the cereal with the milk in the morning. And then he wants a snack at night. The kid has got an appetite, I don't know why. They can eat all day."

Using SNAP to buy food for their children was a common scenario among men that I met who were categorized as single adults without dependents, but who were in fact fathers who did not live with their children. These men reported some of the most severe food hardship of any of the people I encountered, because they often used their meager benefits to fulfill kinship obligations that the welfare administration did not recognize.

Reginald, an African American father of four, lost custody of his children when his apartment building was condemned and he was evicted. He went into the shelter system and subsequently lost his job because the commute and the curfew were unmanageable. He was a regular soup kitchen patron for several months until he got back on his feet. Muscular and well over six feet tall, he looked like a man who liked to eat. During an interview before dinner was served one night at the soup kitchen, he confessed, "I've basically been starving the past three days so my kids could have something to eat. A lot of times I eat a honey bun and some dipsey doodles before bed and that's it. I'm starving now so they can have something later."

I got to know several men in this position because they were regulars at the soup kitchen who looked forward to their "night out" every Wednesday and, often, the only hot meal they ate all week. They often frequented multiple soup kitchens and pantries in order to be able to buy more food for the households where their children lived.

In addition to eating at soup kitchens and getting food from pantries, people often travel in order to save on food purchases. Jimmy would walk from Greenpoint to a less expensive grocery store in Downtown Brooklyn to buy food for his son. "If we go to C Town (a local Greenpoint store), you get two cans of corn for $1.99. If you go to Pathmark, you get two for $1. The kid loves the corn. Got to take the hike. It's cheaper, but it's heavier, and it's a hike, you know what I mean? You save about $20 to $30, but it's a hike."

It takes him about forty-five minutes to walk there and forty-five to walk back. Taking the subway wasn't an option because, as he said, "I ain't got $5 to go there and back." Jimmy ran out of food every month, even though he regularly supplemented by going to soup kitchens and food pantries. "I know a guy who lends me money every now and then. If I borrow $5, I got to pay him back $10, so I try not to do that. But when you're hungry, you got to do it. But I try not to." Saving $5 by walking to the grocery store instead of taking the train meant having money for a meal later in the month. It was the difference between having money to eat one more day and starving or taking on a burdensome debt.

Jimmy worried about his son's well-being and what might happen if there wasn't enough food in the house. "The wife and I will spend whatever we can to keep the food in the house because if ACS [child protective services] comes in, they can take him if there's not a certain amount of food there. A gallon of milk, cereal, eggs, protein, vitamins." Other researchers studying food insecurity have noted that "caregivers are often reluctant to admit that their children may not be getting enough food due to shame or due to the fear that their children might be removed from the home by authorities" (Chilton and Rabinowich 2012, 2, Lee 2010). Given the very real worries that children could be separated from their families if there is not enough food in the house, it is not surprising that these noncustodial fathers went to great lengths to make sure their children could eat.

One of the explicit justifications for welfare reform was to encourage marriage and stable two-parent families as a path out of poverty. The changes in family structure that took place in the latter half of the twentieth century, particularly the rise in divorce rates and single-parent households, created a moral panic that centered on absentee fathers and a welfare state that many argued enabled these changes (Murray 1984, Mead 1986). These critiques were cast in overtly racist terms (Hancock 2004). Despite rising rates of single parent households across racial groups and the fact that the majority of welfare recipients were white, welfare and single-parent households were described as a problem in the Black community. As Dan Quayle famously put it in a speech to the Commonwealth Club in California in 1992, "The anarchy and lack of structure in our inner cities are testament to how quickly civilization falls apart when the family foundation cracks. Children need love and discipline. They need mothers and fathers. A welfare check is not a husband. The state is not a father"(Quayle 1992).

The rhetoric of family values suggested a novel solution to the problem of poverty—dismantling the very programs put in place to provide economic support to poor households. Quayle argued, "We can start by dismantling a welfare system that encourages dependency and subsidizes broken families. We can attach conditions—such as school attendance, or work—to welfare. We can limit the time a recipient gets benefits. We can stop penalizing marriage for mothers. We can enforce child support payments." All of these measures, realized a short four years later in the welfare reform legislation Bill Clinton signed, were designed to promote marriage as a solution to poverty and to impose "personal responsibility" on Black fathers in particular. As Quayle put it, "Failing to support children one has fathered is wrong. We must be unequivocal about this."

Underlying this rhetoric was an assumption that men in particular could and should earn money through work that could be used to support their dependents. The line of logic embodied in Quayle's speech and made manifest in welfare reform legislation rested on the assumption that fathers who fail to provide financially for their children are the root cause of poverty and pathology in poor communities. Jimmy and Reginald's experience suggests that perhaps this logic needs to be reversed. Poverty creates conditions that make parenting far more difficult. When work is out of reach or pays so little that families cannot make ends meet, access to welfare benefits enable men to provide for their children, even if only in small, partial ways.

NETWORKS OF DEPENDENCY

Jimmy drew on family and friends for help and did the same for them when he could. But many of his close relatives and friends were in similar circumstances. He had always tried to help his mom out when he could, and she did the same for him until she went into a nursing home. "She used to send me $20 or $30 every three or four weeks, some cash. But back when I was working, when I had the money, I'd send her some. But now she can't do it no more. And then my brother started helping me, but they cut his hours. He doesn't help me as much as I'd like. Most of the people that I know and see every day are in the same boat I am." Poor and working-class men are part of social networks comprised of people who are facing the same challenges and constraints they are. Though people continue to pool resources across households and engage in reciprocal relationships, economic insecurity strains these networks at multiple junctures. Access to welfare benefits allows men to remain active in these reciprocal relationships and to continue to play the role of provider, if only in a very diminished capacity.

The role these benefits play in maintaining family networks for men has largely been ignored. Welfare legislation has focused on ensuring mothers can provide for their children in the absence of a presumably male provider. The actual social and familial connections that people participate in to sustain themselves have always been more diverse than this ideal nuclear family model—particularly in poor communities (Stack 1974, Coontz 1992). Working-age men are often singled out as people who should be working and are particularly undeserving of assistance. Cutting the benefits of men who "should be working" in an economy that has much less use for these men has ripple effects for the households and family networks they are a part of.

For men, dependency on wages as a means to support a privatized, heterosexual, nuclear family is seen as appropriate. In the United States, our entire social safety net is organized around these "appropriate dependencies" (Fraser and Gordon 1994), shaping networks of distribution within and between households. But this idealized image of work and family has never been a particularly accurate reflection of reality and does not capture the multitude of supportive and reciprocal arrangements that exist, particularly in low-income and queer communities in the United States. Men are embedded in networks of distribution and exchange in their extended families and broader communities as both providers and as dependents.[2] As jobs fail to provide basic subsistence, work as a system of disseminating necessary resources seems increasingly ineffective. There are more than enough material goods to go around, but the politics of distribution based on work, deservingness, and narrow definitions of family are woefully inadequate to meet many people's basic needs (Ferguson 2015).

Single adults like Jimmy are hard hit by work-first welfare policies. Michael Katz has argued that the development of the welfare state in the United States has always been shaped by efforts to make sure that able-bodied adults who can work do work. There is a tremendous amount of suspicion and concern about able-bodied adults getting assistance when they could and should be working to support themselves (Katz 1986). Historically, some exceptions have been made for unemployed women who were needed in the home to care for others, but men have typically been excluded from these exceptions. However, this ideal type, the single, employable man, obscures both the caring and kinship obligations that these men often do take on and the reality of today's informal, flexible labor market that denies these men an identity as a provider, regardless of how desperately they desire or pursue employment. Often the employment they can find is so poorly paid that maintaining those supportive relationships remains key to their survival. Food assistance plays a crucial, if unacknowledged, role in enabling men to maintain reciprocal relationships within their kinship networks. These relationships are often the difference between deep poverty and the abject poverty of the streets.

Unemployed men are the explicit targets of policy makers who want to cut food assistance programs. A story on Fox News, describing an unemployed surfer on food stamps became a talking point for Republican Congress members in their efforts to tighten work requirements for unemployed SNAP recipients (Halloran 2013). As one representative put it, "It is neither right nor fair for those of us who choose to be responsible, taxpaying citizens to pay the way for someone who chooses to make no effort to be productive. So, I don't think it is unreasonable to require someone to work for their benefits." Cutting benefits to these men makes it harder for them to maintain their kinship obligations as they become burdens on the household rather than assets in an era when work is not assured.

As men struggle to find work, they often turn to their familial networks for support. Jesús Garcia, a familiar face from the food pantry line, was forty-eight and lived with his elderly mother a few blocks away from the North Brooklyn Pantry. He had worked in construction most of his life. He came to see me for advice one late summer day. He had been unemployed for over a year after losing a job doing general labor at a warehouse in a nearby neighborhood. He had been on unemployment and

SNAP, and his mother received social security, which kept them afloat while he was out of work.

The trouble started when his unemployment benefits ran out. He received a letter from the welfare office stating that he had to perform a workfare assignment in order to keep his food stamps. Just as he and his mother found themselves in worse economic shape, Jesús became the target of workfare policies that required him to start working for food assistance. New York City was one of only a handful of states and municipalities that continued to enforce time limits for unemployed adults even at the height of the recession. When Mayor Bloomberg first declined the USDA waiver of food stamp work requirements in 2006, he said it was because he was "a firm believer that people should have to work for a living" (Chan 2006). Bloomberg's approach did not soften as unemployment numbers began to rise into the double digits. When the passage of the 2008 stimulus bill revived the issue of work requirements for food stamps, Bloomberg insisted that "nothing had changed" and that they city would continue to deny benefits to anyone out of work who did not participate in a Work Experience Program twenty hours a week. Commissioner Doar said, "The city was ready to expand the Work Experience Program rather than allow people to collect food stamps without working or looking for work" (Bosman 2009). While the food stamp program is almost completely federally funded, the Work Experience Program is not. In essence, the Bloomberg administration insisted on turning down the USDA's waiver and enforcing time limits on unemployed city residents, even though it would be more expensive for the city to do so. This was really quite remarkable in a moment of declining city revenue and calls for fiscal austerity. Though New York City was an outlier at the height of the recession, many states have begun to enforce these time limits once again, kicking the unemployed off of the SNAP rolls. USDA waivers are being revoked nationally as the official unemployment rate drops across the country and some Republican governors have begun to enforce work requirements despite persistently high unemployment (Bolen et al. 2016).

Jesús went to the appointment at the welfare office where they explained that he was going to be assigned to clean the subways in Manhattan for twenty hours a week in exchange for his $200 a month in food assistance. He decided to just walk away. He noted that most people required to work for SNAP assistance refused to do so. "Everyone there just said, forget it. They are not going to work twenty hours a week just for food stamps." The welfare office sanctioned him for failure to comply and he was cut off from SNAP. He was left with no income at all and no food assistance. He felt it was demeaning to have to work for food stamp benefits, but after several months with no benefits and no job he was desperate. Losing his food stamps put a strain on his mother's budget. They came to the pantry each week to pick up food and Jesús ate dinner at the soup kitchen on Wednesday nights. They lived off of his mother's social security, her food stamps, and whatever Jesús could earn from side jobs.

When he came to see me, he had been without food stamps or any real income for three months. He wanted help reapplying for SNAP. After several months without any assistance at all, he was willing to do the workfare assignment. Underlying this policy is a tacit understanding that unemployed adults who receive benefits like food stamps are choosing not to work and must be pushed back into the labor force. In fact, the reality is much more complicated.

What Jesús really wanted was a job. Before we started his food stamp application, he asked me to look at his résumé and we talked through how to explain the gap in his work history. Though he had been looking for work and doing side hustles when he could, he felt no one would hire him at his age. "Once you are almost fifty, nobody wants you because they want someone young they can use and abuse." The work Jesús had done his whole life, general labor and factory work, is a dying industry in New York City. In 1954, the highwater mark for male labor-force participation, the manufacturing and construction sectors accounted for nearly 40 percent of all jobs. Now, after the long decline of manufacturing and the end of the housing bubble, they account for just 13 percent (Bureau of Labor Statistics 2016, Council of Economic Advisors 2016). Men like Jesús, with little education or relevant experience, face particular challenges trying to stay in a labor market that has been radically transformed over the course of their working lives. The occupations that are growing require skills and education that are far out of step with the work histories of men like Jesús. Growing occupations are also deeply gendered. The four occupations expected to add more than one hundred thousand jobs in the next decade—personal care aides, home health aides, medical secretaries, and marketing specialists—all currently have more female workers than male.

Jesús's sole source of security was his close connection with his elderly mother and he was worried about what would happen when she died. He would be homeless if it wasn't for his mother, and, as he put it, "She's not gonna last forever. I worry about that a lot. Like, what am I going to do? I don't want to rob nobody. I don't want to be in the street selling drugs. That's not the kind of person I am. I'm too old for that. I never been to jail. But that's where your mind goes. I've got to eat, I need to take a shower every day, all these little things." His mother also relied on him. She had diabetes and was on a strict diet. Jesús kept her company, cooked for her, helped monitor her health, and took her to her doctors' appointments.

Unable to find work and unable to contribute to his mother's household, Jesús felt compelled to submit to the work requirements in order to receive food stamp benefits. In this case, welfare rules that restrict food aid to the unemployed work hand in hand with a coercive labor market. From the position of the powerful, it is of little consequence whether Jesús chooses to take a low-paid job or submit to a work experience program. He is free to choose, but in the absence of resources for his subsistence, he finds himself in a position—carefully structured by state and market powers—in which he must act. As Barbara Cruikshank points out, "The powers of the powerful depend not so much on the exclusion of the poor as on recruiting and retaining the voluntary compliance of their clients in punitive and coercive programs" (Cruikshank 1999, 37).

What was perhaps most troubling to Jesús was that he was being asked to work "just for food stamps." Requiring people to perform workfare assignments in exchange for food assistance raises a host of questions about the labor rights of welfare recipients, including how they should be paid. Jesús saw these work requirements for what they were, a substandard form of work—a new form of semi-unfree labor.

Other men and women who came to the food pantry and fell into the category of Able-Bodied Adult without Dependent used food stamps to contribute to households where they were staying, sometimes with elderly parents or relatives on a fixed income or with friends. Access to food aid made it possible for them to contribute to a household, and this often meant the difference between staying in the good graces of the person they lived with and wearing out their welcome and being turned out on the street. Cutting off these individuals' food stamp benefits often meant increased food hardship not just for them, but also for their elderly parents or other family members who continued to provide housing for them. In marginal living situations, where people were doubled up and pooling resources, access to food stamps became a buffer, allowing unemployed single men and women to contribute to households and giving them a better chance of staying off the street or out of the shelters.

For Jesús, losing his benefits also strained his ability to care for his mother because they had less food in the house and less control over what they ate. Once his assistance was cut, a lot more of the food they ate was coming from the pantry. Instead of buying food that his mother needed to control her diabetes, they ate whatever the pantry had to offer that week. Food from the pantry varied from week to week in terms of healthiness, sugar content, and quantity. Some weeks we gave out complete bags with frozen chicken, rice, and canned vegetables. Other weeks bags we did the best we could, filling bags with a random assortment of foods that arrived from the food bank.

Reciprocal caring relationships are crucial as rents continue to rise in urban areas.[3] What Jesús feared and Jimmy struggled with was staying off of the streets and out of the shelter system. This ever-present fear loomed large for many of my informants, and not everyone escaped that fate. People's social connections are often the only thing that kept them off the streets. These connections can be extremely fragile—a friend or an acquaintance—and were strengthened by access to public assistance.

In the absence of social or familial connections, and in the face of tenuous access to welfare benefits for the unwaged, people often ended up on the streets or swept up into the carceral system. As Bruce Western points out, unemployed men are most likely to end up in the prison system (Western 2001). Incarceration operates as a labor market institution, containing the disruptive social and economic effects of large numbers of unemployed working-age men who have been left behind in an economy that no longer provides enough jobs for them (Gilmore 2007).

In the years immediately following welfare reform, many women found work in the tight labor markets of the late 1990s. Beginning with the recession in 2000, however, the labor market has been on a downward slide. The employment rate never fully recovered to its pre-recession peak before the new recession started in 2007 (Schmitt 2015). Many of the middle-wage jobs lost in the Great Recession were replaced by low-wage jobs, even as overall employment levels have remained low (National Employment Law Project 2014). Both men and women find themselves in low-wage, part-time, and insecure jobs or out of the labor force entirely. SNAP and welfare policies designed in the 1990s to punish unemployment have not adapted to this new economic reality. The state is no longer the safety net of last resort, making up for failures of the market. Instead, the state has become a super-exploitative employer—requiring men and women to work for far less than they would earn in the private market if they could secure formal employment. Failure to establish a work relationship with a private employer is punished by pushing people into an even more exploitative labor relationship with the state (Collins 2008, Peck 2001). Whereas very poor men were excluded from welfare protections outside of their employment relationships through most of the twentieth century because they were seen as workers and not caretakers, today both men and women are seen primarily as workers. Non-

Exploitation
of state

work has become the basis for exclusion from social protections for both men and women. In the post-gender-based welfare state, both men and women are held to the same punitive social contract—one in which caring labor has been both de-gendered and de-valued.

The commonsense liberal approach, that work can and should be the main mechanism through which goods and services are distributed no longer works for many poor families. This view further ignores the kinds of caring labor performed by both men and women in families and across social networks. Feminists have long argued for the recognition of caring labor carried out by women in the home (James 2012, Federici 2012). Instead, welfare reform delivered a de-gendered welfare state that requires everyone to work, regardless of their caring or kin obligations. While women's abilities to work and provide for dependents has become its own common sense in the twenty-first century, the reality that men can and do provide caring labor for children and others and that this labor can and should be supported has been ignored.

Despite hollow promises to bring back jobs, it seems unlikely that men's employment will have a major turnaround. Recognizing the caring and kinship obligations that men have as both providers and dependents promises to truly de-gender the welfare state. Taking men's caring obligations into account outside the confines of the nuclear family structure offers new ways of thinking about welfare provisions and suggests new kinds of demands for expanding the welfare state. Men and women maintain a myriad of caring, reciprocal relationships. Sometimes they are providers and at other times they are dependents. Recognizing this care work, beyond the limited scope of the patriarchal, nuclear family, and providing support to individuals outside of this limited vision of family is crucial to establishing a safety net for food and other necessities that can meet people's needs.

The crisis of care is deeply enmeshed in and shaped by our work-based safety net. Though caring labor has been devalued through the recalibration of welfare as a work support, the need for care has expanded. Nowhere is this growing need more visible than in the explosion of emergency food programs across the United States.

CHAPTER FIVE

Free to Serve? Emergency Food and Volunteer Labor

I met Fabiola, a forty-five-year-old Puerto Rican woman at the North Brooklyn Pantry the first night I came to volunteer. She had been helping out for about a year and had taken on something of a leadership role among the volunteers. That night, she was overseeing a mix of high school students and community residents. They were filling plastic grocery bags with rice, an array of microwaveable meals that had been market failures, USDA raisins and dates, and a few random canned goods that came from the food bank as donations.

She sat at a table in the back of the church sanctuary at the end of the night, counting her change to see if she had enough money to take the bus home or if she would have to walk. Her apartment was about two miles away and it was a cold November night. She would be back at the pantry the next morning by eight o'clock to help distribute the bags that were being packed as we chatted. She stopped at a nearby convenience store before the pantry opened each week to pick up any leftover food they had. She said she would do more, but she didn't have a car. I marveled at her dedication. She smiled and responded, "It's all love." As we came to be friends over the next two years, my initial impression of Fabiola, as a selfless, dedicated volunteer, gave way to a far more complex picture. What brought Fabiola to the food pantry every week was a mix of altruism, need, fear, and resilience. This love was complicated.

Discourses of care and compassion are central to emergency food providers (EFPs). In the United States, food pantries and soup kitchens are typically thought of as private charities compassionately responding to the needs of the poor. But, as feminist scholars have long pointed out, caring labor (especially the work of feeding families and communities) is more than just compassionate—it is deeply political (Counihan and Kaplan 1998, Van Esterik 1999, Devault 1991, Carney 2015, Kornbluh 2015). Fabiola is a case in point. While her volunteer work is motivated by love for her community, it is also the product of her deep poverty and need. Volunteering at the North Brooklyn Pantry has become an economic lifeline for Fabiola and many other volunteers in the context of weakened welfare protections, widespread economic insecurity, and growing precarity in the United States.

The massive growth of food pantries and soup kitchens in the United States since the 1980s expands opportunities for women like Fabiola to care for their communities. But like all caring labor, volunteer work in soup kitchens and food pantries is shaped by race, class, and gender inequalities (Mullings 1997, Colen 1995, James 2012). Within EFPs, contradictions around how to classify this labor and how it should be remunerated, recognized, and regulated create conflicts between volunteers, clients, and pantry directors. Emergency food providers have become a competitive survival niche for hungry people who

free labor

provide much of the labor soup kitchens and food pantries depend on. By mobilizing large numbers of poor, hungry people as volunteers to distribute surplus food, emergency food providers transform both wasted food and people who are typically considered "burdens" on the state into an important new form of "free labor for a struggling economy"(Adams 2012) in ways that exacerbate entrenched social inequalities.

THE GROWTH OF EFPs

Stagnating wages, insecure work, and threadbare social protections have become prevalent in many industrialized nations in the late twentieth century, leading to increasing economic uncertainty (Standing 2011, Molé 2010, Allison 2012, Kalleberg 2011). Fabiola was intimately aware of these changes in her own life. She was born and raised in North Brooklyn, a working-class neighborhood dominated by factories and run-down tenement housing in the post–World War II period. Married at eighteen, she moved from her parents' house to her husband's in 1985. After a year, she gave birth to her eldest child, a daughter who was born with a severe physical disability. Fabiola had done small jobs off the books and seasonal work at local factories but never had much steady employment. A few years after the birth of her daughter, she and her husband divorced. She applied for welfare, which at the time did not require mothers of young children to perform work assignments in order to qualify for benefits. Six years later, she had another child. She spent their childhoods caring for them, volunteering in their schools and taking her daughter to her numerous doctor and physical therapy appointments.

Fabiola was always poor, but between welfare, a subsidized apartment in public housing, and odd jobs, she was able to keep a roof over her family's head and food on the table. She and I often talked about changes in the neighborhood and the challenges of raising a family as we worked side by side in the pantry. She reflected, "It was much easier to survive and take care of your family back then than it is now. These days it's nearly impossible."

As Fabiola's children grew, both the neighborhood and the city they lived in changed dramatically. Local factories closed and many were renovated into expensive housing as gentrification took hold in the neighborhood. In the 1990s Mayor Rudolph Giuliani instituted some of the most punitive welfare reforms in the country, drastically reducing the welfare rolls in New York City and making it increasingly difficult for poor families to access assistance. As life became more difficult for people like Fabiola and her family, emergency food programs like soup kitchens and food pantries began to proliferate widely. In North Brooklyn there was one small program in the area in 1980. Today there are twelve, with several of these serving well over one thousand people a month. In New York City, the Food and Hunger Hotline, which was organized in 1979, identified 30 emergency food providers. By 1987, that number had grown to 487 and by 1991 the tally was 730 (Poppendieck 1998, 8). Today the Food Bank of New York City, which distributes food to local emergency food providers, serves over one thousand of these institutions.[1] These programs are typically started by and housed in faith-based institutions, senior centers, grassroots community organizations, and increasingly on college campuses.

Feeding America, the nation's largest hunger relief organization, estimates that 46.5 million individuals utilized an emergency food provider (EFP) in 2012, a substantial increase over the 37 million estimated to have used one in 2009 (Malbi et al. 2010, Wienfield et al. 2014).[2] The vast majority of people who access emergency food today rely on it as a regular source of sustenance and, for some households EFPs supply the bulk of the food consumed (Carney 2015, Mares 2013, Wienfield et al. 2014). At the North Brooklyn Pantry, like many EFPs nationally, the vast majority of clients are weekly or monthly customers, depending on how often they are allowed to come and get food (Wienfield et al. 2014). This represents a dramatic change in poor New Yorkers' survival strategies. As Fabiola put it, "I was born and raised in this area and I never knew anything about pantries. I went for myself maybe once or twice years ago with a friend of mine, but I never had the necessity to consistently go."

The expansion of EFPs was not simply a response to growing need in the face of welfare retrenchment and unemployment caused by deindustrialization. It was spurred on by federal funding. Emergency food constitutes a third rail of the contemporary welfare state. While food pantries and soup kitchens existed before 1980, they were typically small and received no regular or reliable state funds. In 1983, Congress passed legislation establishing the Temporary Emergency Food Assistance Program (TEFAP). TEFAP provided funds for the distribution of surplus commodities and, importantly, to reimburse local and private agencies for some administrative costs (Poppendieck 1998, Fitchen 1988). Initially designed as a temporary measure, TEFAP was quickly and continually renewed. In 1990 Congress finally dropped the word "temporary" and renamed the program *The* Emergency Food Assistance Program. This regular infusion of surplus commodities and administrative funding drew ever growing numbers of "community organizations into the food distribution process, and communities without food banks were given a new incentive to develop them." (Poppendieck 1998, 103) It was a very effective incentive.

The explosive growth in the number of EFPs and the number of people served represents what Andrea Muehlebach has called "the opulence of virtue" which "flourishes in proportion to marketization" (Muehlebach 2012, 23). The initial growth in EFPs emerged as direct response to cutbacks to federal entitlements (Dehavenon 1995, Poppendieck 1998). EFPs have become an essential (and expanding) component of the US welfare state, albeit one that obscures state involvement, because these institutions can "do more with less." In response to the increasingly grim economic outlook for the poor and working people since the early 1980s, federal TEFAP funding has unleashed an unprecedented outpouring of care in the form of grocery bags and hot meals and has conjured up an unprecedented volunteer labor force to carry out this work.

Emergency food providers rely heavily on volunteer labor to distribute these resources. Sixty-eight percent of food pantries and 42 percent of soup kitchens in Feeding America's national network report relying entirely on volunteers and have no paid staff. Approximately two million Feeding America network volunteers provided more than 8.4 million hours of service each month in 2012. If these volunteers were paid at the prevailing federal minimum wage of $7.25 per hour, their work would cost more than $60 million in additional monthly wages (Malbi et al. 2010). When I began volunteering at the North Brooklyn Pantry, unpaid volunteers carried out almost all of the day-to-day operations. The church diocese paid Pastor Jon, the pastor at the church where the program was housed, and he used some of his time to order food and oversee the food deliveries each week.

But no one was paid directly for their work with the hunger programs.

Pantries vary widely in the number of paid staff they employ and the larger the pantry is, the more likely they are to have some paid employees. These staff members can be paid from a range of sources, including church funding, private donations, grants, and state funding. At least two of the pantries in North Brooklyn received funding from their local City Council member to pay for a regular staff member and some overhead costs. But even the largest and best-staffed pantries still rely heavily on volunteers. By involving large numbers of community members in these local projects to fight hunger, EFPs give the appearance that they are independent, charitable organizations. But in reality, state funding streams summon volunteers and voluntary efforts into being. Though EFPs appear to come from the heart and not from a mandate, the reality is that most of these institutions could not function without government funding. In New York, federal TEFAP money is supplemented by New York State's Hunger Prevention and Nutrition Assistance Program (HPNAP) and New York City's Emergency Food Assistance Program (EFAP), both of which provide funds to emergency food providers that can be used to purchase food for distribution. However, unlike previous expansions of the welfare state, the jobs produced by this expansion of resources are largely unpaid, unregulated, and unrecognized as employment at all. The enormous growth of volunteer efforts to feed people at the local level represents a broader restructuring of the relationship between the state and local communities. Hunger, once a prominent national issue addressed by the federal government, has been reinscribed as a community issue best responded to by community members.

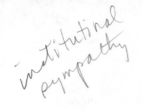
institutional sympathy

LABOR OR LOVE?

EFPs are not organized around a right to adequate food, but on the institutionalization of sympathy—the sympathetic response to need. These shoe-string operations do the best they can with what they have, but they often run out of food and have to turn people away (Koible and Stampas 2016). Pantry staff and volunteers care deeply about hunger, but EFPs are organized in ways that ensure these institutions cannot fully meet the needs of the people who rely on them. Volunteers play a crucial role in deflecting the demands of clients who need more than EFPs can provide. As Andrea Muehlebach argues, "Compassionate labor operates not as a mitigating force against, but as a vehicle for the production and maintenance of a new exclusionary order" (Muehlebach 2011). In the public imagination, volunteers are moved to help out of a sense of compassion, rather than by a paycheck. The proper response is gratitude.

Volunteers and pantry clients often resolved conflicts that erupted as food was being distributed through appeals to this sense of appropriate gratitude. It was not unusual for pantry clients to complain about the food that was being given out or their treatment by a particular volunteer. Volunteers joked among themselves about the daily complaints, often dismissing them by pointing out, "It's not like we get paid to put up with all this." Food pantry clients, for their part, would often intervene when they heard other people on the line complaining, reminding them that the volunteers who hand out food "don't need to be doing this."

However, many volunteers do, in fact, need to be doing this work in order to make ends meet in their own households. The core volunteers who showed up every week and did the bulk of the work at the North Brooklyn Pantry were generally older, unemployed, or marginally employed women and a few men. These core volunteers depended heavily on what they could take home with them from the pantry each week. With almost no income, Fabiola needed the food she took home with her every week. Like many of the other volunteers, coming in to pack bags and hand out groceries also meant she could pick and choose what she needed for her own kitchen (see alsoCarney 2015, 186). Though this wasn't her plan, volunteering at the pantry had become Fabiola's lifeline. "I never thought a year or two years later that this is where I would be. My pay comes in my food and I really am okay." Fabiola's dedication, coming in every week, was a response to deep and devastating food insecurity. She quite literally worked for food and missing "work" for a week would mean not eating.

There was a tacit understanding at the pantry that the people helping out sometimes took a little extra food for themselves. There were five core pantry volunteers who came each week. While other volunteers would come occasionally and help out, these women were the backbone of the operation. Angela was a single, middle-aged Puerto Rican woman who had lived in the neighborhood her whole life. She and her adopted daughter lived off of a small disability allowance, food stamps, and a stipend she received as a foster parent. She never missed a week at the pantry and was reprimanded several times for taking too much food home with her at the end of the day. Katherine, Ana, and Grace were all retirees who received social security and helped to support their extended families. They stocked their kitchens with what they could take home from the pantry. And then there was Fabiola, who had virtually no income at all. She did informal work as a party planner, organizing salsa nights and other events, but she earned very little from these efforts. Fabiola insisted on living life on her own terms, despite the pressure she felt to conform to social expectations that she should work. Katherine was especially critical of her, wondering why she didn't just get a job. But Fabiola did not see how the kinds of jobs she would be able to get, as a cashier or a housecleaner, would really improve her life. For her, helping out at the food pantry and cobbling together what she could from odd jobs might mean she was always broke, but it also meant she controlled her own time.

> I feel that physically and financially I'm better off bein' the poor person that I am right now and surviving. In the long run, there's the money on one hand. But it'll be gone in the next. Yeah, I know people would think that's a cop-out. Well, you should work or whatever. Your kids are big or whatever. It's not a point of what I should do or shouldn't do.... I'd rather scrimp and struggle than to bust my ass working, working, working and my body's dyin'. And to just give my money away, what's the point? You could give me a metro card and food and I'm fine. I am so fine with that. Other people don't see it that way. Money doesn't buy happiness, so no matter how much money you have and you pay all your bills, that doesn't mean you're a happy camper.

Fabiola saw that the kinds of work available to her, as a middle-aged woman with little work experience and only a high school diploma, as a heavy burden that offered very little reward. She would be stuck in that segment of the working poor, busting their ass and still hovering at the poverty line. So, she rejected formal work and pursued an income doing the things she loved, volunteering at the food pantry, organizing parties and salsa nights, making scrapbooks for a small fee, raffling off a bottle of liquor at the club.

Fabiola was not opposed to work. She consistently went above and beyond at the pantry, earning her role as the de facto volunteer supervisor after just a few short months helping out. "I would come in the morning and things just started gradually changing, and I just kept giving suggestions and (Pastor Jon) was OK with them as long as they worked, and a lot of them did work. I believe for the most part we run more effectively now than we did when I started as a volunteer." Fabiola, more than anyone I met during my time at the North Brooklyn Pantry, refused work in the formal labor market. But her refusal was "not a rejection of productive activity per se, but rather a refusal of central elements of the wage relation and those discourses that encourage our consent to the modes of work that it imposes" (Weeks 2011, 124). In refusing the kinds of low paid, insecure work available to her, she rejected "work's domination over the times and spaces of life and of its moralization, a resistance to the elevation of work as necessary duty and supreme calling" (124). Volunteering at the pantry allowed Fabiola to do the kind of labor that mattered to her, caring for her community, even if this work was essentially unpaid.

Conflicts often erupted among the volunteers over who could take what from the pantry and how food was distributed. I gave Fabiola a ride home one night after a long day at the pantry. She was complaining about Ana taking food out of the bags that were already packed. We packed two kinds of bags each week. One set was the regular bags for people who had a kitchen where they could cook. The special bags contained only ready-to-eat items like bread and cereal and were for people who were homeless or had no kitchen. Ana had taken cans of tuna from the special bags and encouraged two new volunteers to take some as well. Fabiola was bothered by Ana's actions and was fuming on the ride home. For her, taking food from the special bags was a line that should not be crossed. "You know, we all need. I need. But don't take from those guys."

The lines between compensating oneself, taking too much, and stealing were very blurry and constantly policed by the volunteers. Fabiola explained that taking food was OK because "that's all we get, what we take." But all the volunteers worried about people overdoing it and calling attention to either the pastors or other pantry clients, who, they feared, might report the pantry to city authorities. For their part, the pastors were aware that the most dedicated volunteers relied heavily on food from the pantry and that their need ensured that the pantry had a regular, reliable labor force each week. However, explicitly acknowledging this arrangement was impossible. Nonprofit organizations have to comply with wage and hour laws, like any other employer. Fabiola's view of herself as a quasi-employee whose "pay comes in food" was in direct contradiction to the legal definition of a volunteer who performs services for a non-profit entity without compensation. For Fabiola and the other volunteers, working at the North Brooklyn Pantry was an important part-time gig in an economy where informal, unregulated labor has become widespread (Sassen 1994). Part of the job was maintaining the illusion that these women were truly volunteers, acting selflessly, while hiding or ignoring the degree to which they depended on this work to fulfill their material needs.

It was common to meet retired men and women living on fixed incomes or people who were unemployed volunteering at pantries. Javier, the unpaid director of another small pantry in the area described how he was able to staff his organization. "I can't give stipends or a tip to the person downstairs who is giving the food. He was two years on unemployment, so he was able, for the time he was on unemployment, to help me. There's another lady doing the same thing now. But what is going to happen when the unemployment is over? I don't know. And then each year it's a little less support from public funding, less support from church funding." For all of these men and women, their participation as volunteers was structured by their relationships to the labor market and to various social welfare programs. When they lose jobs, or social security does not pay enough for rent and groceries, soup kitchens and food pantries provide access to needed resources.

Volunteers also gain access to valuable forms of social standing. Though the need that motivates many volunteers to come to the pantry each week is often no different than the need that brings clients, the difference between giving and receiving is no small matter. Stacey McCarthy, who helps oversee HPNAP grants for several hundred pantries in New York City, observed, "I've seen it at every pantry. There's a contentious relationship. It's like the lucky few who are giving it out. And then you get the lucky volunteers who may have been people pulled off the line to help out." Becoming a volunteer, as opposed to a client, means that you have access to more food not only for yourself, but to distribute among family and friends. This dichotomy, between those "on the line" and the lucky few who are allowed to help reflects the broader dichotomy of emergency food. Volunteers are transformed from objects of pity into people who can pity. To go back on the line after being inside is unthinkable. It is a demotion because as volunteers they have the ability to distribute resources in ways that directly contribute to their economic survival. Helping family and friends was a way to strengthen reciprocal relationships that have long sustained poor households and communities (Stack 1974, Caldwell 2004). Emergency food has become a competitive survival niche for the very poor, particularly those few who are invited in "off the line" to become volunteers.

The core volunteers at the North Brooklyn Pantry all had deep ties in the neighborhood. As volunteers, they played important roles in their social networks, distributing extra food to family and friends. The first few weeks that I volunteered I was oblivious to these exchanges. I would often pick up bags of frozen chicken or extra milk and ask why these were tucked under a pew in the sanctuary of the church, only to be told by one of the other volunteers that they were for a cousin or a friend who was coming by later. Other pantry clients worked to establish relationships with volunteers by offering gifts or small tokens of appreciation. Rarely a week went by without someone bringing a homemade dessert or cups of coffee for the volunteers in an attempt to curry favor with the women handing out the food.

But there were limits to volunteers' informal compensation. When it became egregious or impossible to ignore, the pastors had to enforce the rule that no one was supposed to take more than what the clients on the line received, no matter how dedicated the volunteer in question was. Angela was by far the most aggressive at taking food. She often filled her shopping cart to the brim for her own kitchen and loaded her close family members with extra bags of groceries when they came to the pantry. After several warnings, Angela was finally asked to leave. Her dismissal rattled the remaining volunteers. Their positions as valued volunteers no longer felt secure. There was a sense that everyone needed to be more cautious and restrained in taking food and giving preference to others.

VOLUNTEER LABOR AND WORK-FIRST WELFARE

Most volunteers relied on several resources, including social security, food stamps, informal work, and help from family and friends in addition to what they took from the food pantry. Fabiola had talked to me for months about applying for food stamps, weighing the pros and cons, and worrying about whether it would cause problems with her housing or her health care. After years in the welfare system, Fabiola was hesitant to apply. In her assessment, getting food from the pantry was far more stable and less risky than engaging with a welfare system designed to enforce labor market participation and to punish unemployment (Dickinson 2016, Collins and Mayer 2010, Peck 2001). She feared the stringent work requirements associated with welfare. As she put it, "The system has changed so much. I could go back to welfare right now, but if they're going to put me to work in a place and cleaning up trucks, no, I'm sorry. It's not that I'm better than that, it's just that I can do more." I tried to assure her that food stamps were different, but she wasn't convinced. She was poor, but her life was stable. She worried that applying for SNAP could have unintended consequences.

> Sometimes you're like is it worth it? When you're in that peaceful place, you don't wanna disrupt it. Because all it takes is one little thing. And that could just escalate into I don't know what. I guess that would be my biggest fear. I don't wanna mess up what I have, which is not much. But my home means everything to me. So as long as I can pay my rent and my light—I'm not talking about buying food or buying clothes or going anywhere. My rent and my light are important. The rest will come. That's why I come here and deal with the crap a lot a time. I need my stuff. I gotta go. So that's it.

Sensing that her position at the pantry might not be entirely secure after Angela was asked to leave, however, she changed her mind. After several years of not being able to go to the grocery store to purchase food, she told me, "I might as well do the food stamps. I want to be able to go to the supermarket and buy something." We submitted her application and several weeks later she was approved. She described going to the grocery store for the first time with her food stamp card and picking out some meat. When she took it up to the cash register her eyes welled up with tears. The cashier asked her if she was ok. Fabiola, pretending to wipe tears away as she told me the story, said she replied, "I'm just so happy."

A month or so later, Fabiola pulled me aside with a worried look as soon as I got the pantry. She handed me a letter from the welfare office, requiring her to come in for a work assessment. She was beside herself. "This is why I didn't want to do this. I'm not gonna clean up the park," she whispered so that the other volunteers couldn't hear. I had been helping people apply for several months before Fabiola decided to apply, and I had never seen a letter requiring SNAP recipients to report for a work assignment. I knew the rule was on the books in New York City, but from what I had heard from other food stamp advocates around the city it had been enforced sporadically. I knew Fabiola was taking a risk in applying, but I was still surprised when I saw the letter. Unbeknownst to me, New York City's welfare offices had recently begun enforcing this rule more stringently just as Fabiola had applied for SNAP.[3]

In New York City, unemployed food stamp applicants were now regularly being assigned to the Work Experience Program (WEP). Fabiola saw engaging with the welfare system, whether for food stamps or for cash assistance, as a threat to her incredibly meager, but stable situation. She was willing to suffer serious hardships, including having almost no income and struggling with severe food insecurity, in order to avoid what she saw as a destabilizing and demeaning system of work requirements. At the same time, being able to go to the store and choose her own food literally brought tears to her eyes after two years of eating whatever the food pantry had to offer.

Fabiola's worry was palpable and I felt a sense of responsibility for convincing her to apply for SNAP. We spent the afternoon debating how to handle the situation. Pastor Jon suggested we write a letter to the welfare office explaining that Fabiola was a volunteer and that her work at the pantry ought to count as her work assignment. As Jon noted, "people who have to do WEP assignments are one of our most reliable forms of labor around here." While volunteers like Angela were admonished for treating volunteering as a job and compensating themselves with food, this same labor was treated as an appropriate "work activity" when the welfare office assigned welfare applicants to these tasks. Poor people who apply for cash assistance and are subject to work requirements are frequently assigned to do voluntary service at a nonprofit like a food pantry.[4] Fabiola was skeptical about whether the welfare office would accept a letter from Pastor Jon and allow her to stay at the North Brooklyn Pantry. After years of negotiating the system, she was unconvinced that the welfare office would let her choose her own work assignment. Ultimately Fabiola, who had serious back problems, was able to submit a letter from her doctor saying she was not fit for employment and was given an exemption from the work requirements. This exemption had an enormous impact on her ability to feed herself, significantly alleviating her experience of hunger and food insecurity. It also allowed her to maintain control over her own labor as a volunteer.

VOLUNTEER LABOR AND SOCIAL INEQUALITY

Fabiola's experience illuminates something about the kinds of labor regimes that are emerging out of the growth of EFPs. Poor women like Fabiola are caught up by the ironies of the current economy. There is a shortage of decent work for all the people who want it and work conditions have deteriorated steadily for low-skill workers like Fabiola and Angela, who have only high school educations and limited work experience (Kalleberg 2011). Both of these women dedicated their lives to providing caring labor to others. Fabiola's choice to care for her daughter left her with few options for entering the workforce after her daughter was grown. Angela was the sole caregiver to her adopted daughter who was disabled and required constant supervision. At the same time, the growth of the voluntary efforts to feed the poor gave these women the opportunity to create a job for themselves, one where they could, like many informally employed workers, "determine the schedule, pace, and intensity" of their work (Millar 2008). They were engaged in what James Ferguson terms "a kind of improvisation under conditions of adversity" that characterizes the precarious livelihoods of the very poor (Ferguson 2015). But, like so many informally employed workers, Fabiola could not represent this labor as a job to welfare officials in a way that would exempt her from work requirements, much like poor women can no longer represent the care of their own children as socially valued work. Emergency food providers have engaged women like Fabiola and Angela in a form of caring labor that is socially valued precisely because it is not financially valued.

Susan Hyatt argues that "neoliberal governance masks the withdrawal of public resources from all communities by making volunteerism an obligation of citizenship for the working and middle classes, while simultaneously diminishing the significance of volunteerism in poor communities toward the end of creating an extremely low-paid workforce (Hyatt 2001, 288). Fabiola and Angela's volunteerism were diminished by their need. However, contemporary urban governance is characterized by more than just the *withdrawal* of public resources. New kinds of resources and funding produce novel institutions, like food banks, food pantries and soup kitchens. Hyatt's argument that voluntarism masks the effects of austerity cannot properly explain the massive growth of EFPs in the last three decades, particularly since state funding is what brought these institutions into being. In the name of efficiency, new forms of public resources come into being that are socially valued because they can "do more with less" and, in the case of EFP's, do so by mobilizing hungry people to do the work of distributing these resources. This arrangement saves the state substantial funds in actually paying people to do this work. Further, it creates value out of both surplus food and surplus labor in the form of good feeling and new forms of public recognition for poor women like Fabiola.

At the same time, food pantries are, quite literally, the embodiment of a failed welfare apparatus and a failed labor market to provide sufficient resources to poor people living in the United States. They occupy the negative space of welfare and work—the spaces of human need that are no longer filled by these regulatory institutions. Volunteers, often desperately poor themselves, are the workforce maintaining an enormous network of EFPs that does more than just distribute meals and groceries for the poor. They produce good feeling. In an era when providing for the poor is no longer understood as a collective social responsibility, but a voluntary choice, "giving back" by volunteering in one's own community becomes a mode of establishing citizenship and belonging. But as Fabiola and Angela's experience shows, these new forms of recognition are tenuous at best. Where middle-class volunteers really do act freely, poor New Yorkers need to do this work in order to access resources for themselves and their families. The poorest and most marginalized are often assigned to volunteer as a condition of receiving welfare benefits, often in places they do not choose and where they do not have personal connections. These "volunteers" lose even the modest benefits of unpaid volunteer work, including determining one's own work schedule and choosing where to volunteer. If they become too reliant on pantry resources they can be dismissed or reprimanded.

This becomes a public expression of who has the right to care for their communities. Struggles over who can volunteer to feed the poor and on what terms reflects the raced and classed struggles of women of color and poor women who have long fought for the right to care for their own children (Mullings 1995, 1997, Colen 1995). Women like Fabiola and Angela have long been engaged in unpaid caring labor. But, like the private care of children and families, poor women's public contributions to their communities are carefully regulated and controlled. Poor women like Fabiola are celebrated as volunteers only so long as they can maintain the illusion that they are giving freely, from the heart. Once they ask for something in return—food stamps in Fabiola's case and food from the pantry in Angela's—their need erases their service.

Because these women could not claim an identity as a worker—the identity they were expected to assume as a poor, single woman—both their service and their need were subject to intense scrutiny. Fabiola became a burden to the state despite her volunteerism when she applied for food stamps. In this way, the growth of EFPs brings into being new kinds of inequalities. For Fabiola, her chosen role as a volunteer was part of the "scramble for recognition" where "citizens wrangle over the right to work" (Muehlebach 2012, 227), even when this work is unpaid. Food programs, where volunteers pay themselves by choosing their own food, are a socially valued avenue for poor women to access needed household resources. However, the kind of public, caring labor carried out by volunteers is shot through with new kinds of inequalities, including who is able to take on these socially valued labors and under what conditions. For the poor and unemployed, engaging with the welfare system can transform one's service into an obligation. For poor women like Fabiola and Angela who are "there because they need," expressing love and care through community service is complicated by their own hunger and poverty.

What Fabiola's experience begins to illuminate is the myriad ways that the growth of pantries and the ways these resources are used by community members are both intricately tied to the labor market and to welfare policy. Emergency Food Providers, structured by state funding, but not identifiable as state institutions, are inextricably linked to both the market and the state. People come to rely on them to varying degrees dependent on their integration into the labor market and/or the safety net.

The remarkable growth in these institutions—from thirty in 1980 to over a thousand today in New York City—have become an institutionalized form of crisis management. There is a self-perpetuating cycle at the heart of funding for emergency food providers: the intensification of poverty creates more need, which creates more demand. Emergency food providers document this increasing demand and lobby for more funding. As the need expands, food banks get more efficient at dealing with it. In doing so, they employ more volunteers, often hungry people themselves who may choose or may be obligated by the welfare office to do this work. This cycle, however, does not address the root causes of hunger. In the process, new consumption patterns and new forms of labor emerge. There is a political economy of virtue that poor people, donors, and nonprofits all depend on that is comprised of growing need and measurable response and that produces a tremendous amount of free labor to fulfill growing and urgent social needs. But the degree to which this labor is freely given is shaped by raced, classed, and gendered exclusions built into the waged labor market and the welfare systems.

These exclusions have real consequences for individuals and families struggling on the edge of food insecurity who are particularly vulnerable to diet-related disease and poor health. Narratives of food and health are frequently invoked by policy makers to justify the expansion of food assistance as a nutrition program. However, as we will see in the next chapter, the rhetoric of nutrition is hampered by the realities of the food safety net.

political economy
of virtue

CHAPTER SIX

No Free Lunch

*The Limits of Food Assistance as a Public
Health Intervention*

Mayor Michael Bloomberg rose to national prominence for his
innovative and sometimes controversial public health policies in
New York City. Bloomberg, a billionaire who made his fortune
as a media mogul, sold himself to New Yorkers as a CEO who
could improve the city by running it as effectively as he had run
his media empire. One of his primary concerns throughout his
administration was reversing the so-called obesity epidemic
(Barnhill 2011). He was an early proponent of the idea that public
policy could be leveraged to address rising rates of obesity and
diet-related disease. In addition to a range of novel policy innovations, including banning trans fats in restaurants, attempting
to ban the sale of large sodas in New York City, and attempting
to ban SNAP recipients from buying soda, Bloomberg's administration saw expanding food stamps as a way to improve the
health and nutrition of low-wage New Yorkers. As one Bloomberg appointee who worked closely on food issues told me, "We
consider everything, primarily, from a public health angle,"
including the push to enroll more New Yorkers in the SNAP

program. Bloomberg bragged about increased enrollment in SNAP during his tenure. Food stamp rolls rose 120 percent during his twelve years in office. This growth was no accident. Much of it came before the onset of the 2007 economic crisis and was due at least in part to policy shifts by the Bloomberg administration that eased access to food stamps. From a low of eight hundred thousand recipients in 2000, the food stamp caseload reached nearly 1.1 million by December 2004 and soared to 1.8 million by 2012.

At the same time, Bloomberg maintained a hard-line commitment to work-first welfare policy. During the recession, New York City was one of the only places in the United States that refused to accept the blanket waiver to the food stamp work requirements offered by the Obama administration in the face of high levels of unemployment across the country. As we have seen, work requirements made it harder for some New Yorkers to access food assistance, practically ensuring that the quality of their diets would suffer. On the surface, his administration's approach to SNAP, promoting expanded access to food stamps to improve public health while also maintaining restrictions that made it harder for some New Yorkers to afford food, seems paradoxical. His contradictory stance on SNAP policy only makes sense in light of Bloomberg's broader governing philosophy.

Both his concerns over public health and a staunch commitment to work-first welfare reflect Bloomberg's conception of the city as a corporate entity (Brash 2011). In an interview early on in his first term, Mayor Bloomberg reflected, "I've spent my career thinking about the strategies that institutions in the private sector should pursue, and the more I learn about this institution called New York City, the more I see the ways in which it needs to think like a private company. Successful companies figure out which customers they have a chance to get and which customers, if they get them, will contribute to their bottom line" (Cardwell 2003).

Bloomberg's approach, imagining the city as a business and running it as such, meant viewing the working class primarily as employees instead of citizens. Running the city like a private company meant rewarding citizens who contribute to the city's brand and transforming or excluding those who do not. He saw poverty policy as a way to produce desirable citizens at the very bottom of the income scale. His administration's response to intra-urban competition was to pursue policies that transformed New York into a good place to do business, including the cultivation of a compliant, healthy, low-wage labor force catering to every imaginable need of the urban elite—as nannies, dog walkers, food service workers, delivery men and women, baristas, and nail technicians.

The fact that these workers often don't earn enough to afford healthy food hurts the city's bottom line in a few ways. Bloomberg saw the long-term health costs and lost productivity associated with poor diets as something that must be appropriately managed. One way to manage these social costs was by subsidizing low wages with food stamps to encourage healthier eating. Low-wage workers were a key constituency who were cared for as useful human capital contributing to the city's bottom line. Unemployed New Yorkers, on the other hand, offered nothing of value. Restricting their access to food stamps unless they joined the labor market was simply a way of pushing them off the city's balance sheet.

Bloomberg's concern with obesity and chronic illness reflected a widespread view that poor health is best understood in market terms. Diet-related disease is described as "a serious and *costly* health problem facing our nation, costing $152 billion in direct medical costs annually and $73 billion in indirect costs from lost productivity, higher insurance premiums and absence from work" (American Public Health Association 2013). Chronic illnesses like diabetes, heart disease, and hypertension disproportionately impact poor New Yorkers, and Blacks and Latinos are affected at higher rates than whites (Kim, Berger, and Matte 2006). Many of the initiatives in New York City and across the nation to reduce obesity explicitly link poverty, eating habits, and fiscal health. These linkages are made particularly clear in this passage from a *New York Times* article on the growing epidemic of type 2 diabetes in New York City: "The work force 50 years from now is going to look fat, one-legged, blind, a diminution of able-bodied workers at every level presuming that current trends persist." The article goes on to warn, "These people will not be able to function in society without significant aid" (Kleinfield 2006). Poor people's consumption has emerged as a new kind of threat to the imagined future of the city and the nation. The obesity epidemic and the high rates of diabetes in New York and across the United States are framed as endangering the productivity of the future workforce while costing the state through publicly funded health expenditures. In response, Bloomberg made reducing obesity and chronic diet-related disease a centerpiece of his administration.

Just as important as the projected health costs are concerns over a growing segment of the population that won't be able to contribute to society through work in the future. As large numbers of people become incapacitated from what are often perceived as diseases caused by lifestyle choices, these lifestyles increasingly become something that must be governed. Bloomberg made several attempts to shape the consumption habits of the poor. Robert Doar, the commissioner for human services told me, "Bloomberg has transformed the food stamp program, doubling enrollment since the time he came into office. It's more than a welfare program, but a work support. Bloomberg came in and the numbers went up because he talked about it as a work support." At the same time, the commissioner complained, "It's called the supplemental nutrition assistance program, but it's not doing enough on nutrition. We want to do more." One of the things Bloomberg wanted to do was to ban the use of food stamps for the purchase of sugary soda, but the US Department of Agriculture (USDA) turned down this request. Doar lamented, "We just wanted to try it." Bloomberg's attempts to shape food aid as a nutrition program and a public health intervention are motivated by concerns about the high social costs of cheap, unhealthy foods. However, his administration's approach demonstrates the limits of food assistance as a public health intervention concerned first and foremost with the city's fiscal health.

AT THE WHIM OF THE GROCERY STORE

In the face of what has often been defined as a national obesity epidemic, individuals are understood as responsible for their own health, largely through their eating decisions and behavior. As Julie Guthman points out, the conventional wisdom that rapid changes in body size over the past several decades are caused primarily by overconsumption of calories and lack of exercise has become hegemonic primarily because it fits neatly into a political economic context that relies on individualization and individual choice. Citizens have a responsibility to maintain their health so that they don't become a burden to society (Guthman 2011). "By unquestioningly connecting "obesity and overweight" to risky health behaviors, medical professionals and public health spokespersons categorize them as "preventable illnesses," which means that people who are fat are willfully creating the social and physical costs" (Julier 2013, 554). Underlying the national push to shame, cajole, and transform fat bodies is an understanding of economic citizenship as a duty to be productive and add to (not subtract from) the overall economy.

In this context, citizens are tasked with a new form of labor—the job of staying thin, losing weight, and maintaining work-ready bodies as a form of potential human capital—in the face of a consumer market that inundates consumers with unhealthy food at every turn (and makes vast profits in doing so). However, people do this labor of self-improvement and self-monitoring under radically different conditions, depending on their income, employment status, educational level, and access to resources—all of which are shaped by entrenched racial, class, and gender inequalities. The prevalence of cheap unhealthy food, low-wage labor, and exclusionary welfare policies conflicts with the real health needs of a low-income population that cannot afford to self-regulate in the way that more affluent Americans do. This was certainly the case for Stephanie Figlia, a thirty-seven-year-old white woman who was a regular at the North Brooklyn Pantry.

The first time I interviewed Stephanie, she described her family's struggles with food insecurity. Her family received SNAP, but it wasn't enough to cover all of their food expenses. She described cutting back on meals and buying the cheapest foods in the supermarket to make sure that her five-year-old son would have something to eat. "Within two weeks, we're already *food availability* (handwritten note)

rationing. I'm tellin' my son, no. I'm givin' him toast and jelly, Ramen noodles, nothing that's very healthy that I would normally feed us. That's where most of my weight gain came in. The less-healthier food is a little bit cheaper. So of course, you're gonna gain weight on that. That's not gonna help ya any. So, what they're giving us is not helping. We just make do."

Her family had experienced a long slide from working-class stability to an uncertain life on public assistance—something Stephanie described as "a nightmare." It all started when her husband, Dominic, a white man in his mid-thirties who worked in construction, lost his job. She had been working full-time as a customer service representative supervisor. Between unemployment and food stamps, they were able to make ends meet, scraping together rent money each month for their small two-bedroom apartment in Long Island. Dominic took the opportunity to get his commercial driver's license, but it didn't improve his job prospects. Dominic has a criminal record, which makes finding employment more difficult. They dipped into their savings to cover expenses until that was gone. Then Stephanie got laid off. As she put it, "That was it. It was the end of the road."

They moved in with a friend in Brooklyn who offered to let them stay until they got back on their feet, and they applied for public assistance. Over the next few months, Stephanie and Dominic struggled to keep their family fed, but they often found themselves without enough to eat. As their economic situation deteriorated, Stephanie had to adjust the way they shopped and cooked. She often reminisced about meals they would make when they were still living in Long Island—chicken and sautéed spinach, bacon and eggs for breakfast, or homemade pizza with extra cheese. "Having choices is now a luxury. The types of choices we could make before are not there." Many pantry

Eating at the whim of the grocery store.

Solid

clients struggled with the lack of choice and the knowledge that what they were eating was not good for their long-term health. One middle-aged regular at the North Brooklyn Pantry poignantly explained, "I eat at the whim of the grocery store. Whatever's on sale, that's what I eat."

Like so many in her situation, Stephanie found herself rationing the cheapest foods she could find. In the absence of steady, sufficient income, Stephanie's eating habits represented both a survival strategy and a risk. She relied heavily on modern-day proletarian hunger killers, like ramen noodles and saltine crackers so she and her family could, as she put it "just have something in our stomachs" (Mintz 1995; Errington, Fujikura, and Gewertz 2012). Public health experts have consistently linked cheap food to poor health (Darmon and Drewnoski 2008). For Stephanie, cheap food was both a problem and a solution. Cheap foods like instant noodles kept her family from starving. But they did so at a cost. Stephanie had put on weight eating this way and she worried about her family's long-term health. For her, the links between health, poverty, and food assistance were tangible and immediate. However, the solutions being offered by the Bloomberg administration did little to help her act on her health concerns.

WORK-FIRST WELFARE AND FOOD INSECURITY

Work rules kept Stephanie's family mired in severe food insecurity for months. Her attempts to "just make do" with cheap, unhealthy foods took a toll on her family's health and well-being. Because of a bureaucratic error on the part of the welfare office, her family was given food stamps and cash assistance for a family of two rather than the budget for a family of three. They got $264 a month in cash and $300 in food stamps. One of the primary reasons her family's struggle with food insecurity was so severe was because of the mistake the welfare office made.

Stephanie had tried several times, beginning in June, to fix the situation with her family's public assistance and have Dominic put on the case so they could get food stamps for him, which would help alleviate their food shortage. Each time she was told that it would be taken care of only to discover the next month when the benefits were put on her card that it hadn't been. This kind of bureaucratic disentitlement, where agency error prevents people from accessing benefits, was a common experience at the welfare office for poor families, particularly those who were unemployed. As Stephanie put it, "Nobody's there to help you. They want to make the system hard. They don't want nobody on it. They want to weed out all the people who are taking advantage, who get frustrated and don't come back."

Their struggles with food insecurity were shaped by welfare state policies that withheld food from families in order to encourage work. When her family moved to Brooklyn and applied for public assistance, both she and Dominic were unemployed. Stephanie was given an exemption from work requirements because of her chronic depression, but Dominic was immediately assigned to the Back to Work program, a job training and placement program required by HRA in order to qualify for cash benefits. After two and a half months of attending Back to Work forty hours a week, sitting in classes and filling out résumés, Dominic still had not received any benefits. He and Stephanie were living on a tiny budget for a family of two and trying to find work. In order to make ends meet, they sold clothes, toys and other household goods. Dominic occasionally did odd jobs for a doctor whose office was on their block, but he found he had to turn him down in order to go to the Back to Work Program most days. He was angry and frustrated that he had to turn down small jobs that could put cash in his pocket in order to attend a job placement program that was not helping him find work.

The stress of their situation was overwhelming. Though getting food from food pantries helped, there was never enough food in the house for all three of them. During one of our first interviews, she confessed, "Sometime I go without or eat once a day. My son has school. I know that at least he's gettin' breakfast and lunch. I don't have to worry. But now I have to worry because I have the baby." At this point, Stephanie's voice started breaking up and she could barely hold back the tears. She was three months pregnant at the time of our interview. At thirty-seven, she felt this was probably her last chance to have another child. But it couldn't have happened at a more difficult time. She continued, "I can't just eat once a day. I have to eat healthy for her."

The disentitlement and disruptions families face come in the form of both agency neglect and official policy. In late August, Dominic was sanctioned for failing to dress properly for his Back to Work assignment. Though they had never received any assistance for him, he was now being cut from their case. Stephanie explained, "at the Back to Work program, they wanted them to come in with slacks, dress shoes, button-down shirts, ties, all this stuff. Dominic doesn't have these. He's been in general labor all his life. He told them that. They sent him down to a church that had hand-me-down clothes, but the church didn't have business attire. When he returned to the program the next day, the woman at the front desk wouldn't swipe him in because he had jeans on. He was wearing the nicest clothes he owned— dark jeans and polo shirt." When he was finally allowed in to see catch 22

his case manager, she told him to go home and change. He told her he would come back with similar clothes so she sanctioned him for failure to comply. Dominic was beside himself. He was doing is best to comply because he needed the help. Despite his efforts, he was prevented from complying because of strict, unwavering adherence to somewhat arbitrary rules.

Stephanie was incredulous. After weeks of attending this program and getting no help, Dominic was now being sanctioned. "First of all, they're sanctioning' him. He's never even been on the case. I haven't even gotten anything. He's been goin' to this thing. I haven't got one penny, one food stamp, one nothing for him. He has no Medicaid or nothin'. End of the month, we're rationing. We have nothing. It's bad." Between the sanction and the bureaucratic errors, Dominic was not added to his family's SNAP case until February. In the meantime, they had to move out of their friend's building and go into the shelter system, something Stephanie had been trying to avoid for months.

Moving people from welfare to work was the mantra of welfare reform. Sanctions are intended to push people into the labor market by reducing dependency on state benefits and inducing "responsible" job ready behaviors and attitudes. However, Stephanie and Dominic's hardships were not caused by a failure to be job ready. They were both desperate for work and would take whatever they could get. Stephanie got a seasonal position at Kmart before the holidays and jumped at the opportunity to work again, despite there being little hope of it turning into permanent employment. She was willing to take anything just to make some money for her family. We often met at the public library where she spent her days sending out job applications while her son was in school. "Once this all happened, I applied to McDonald's. I applied to White Castle. I will take two minimum-wage jobs if I have to. You're overqualified. You're this. You don't get the callbacks. You don't get nothing. I'll start from the bottom again. Even though my mental state's really not right, I have no choice but to find something."

Work framed everything Stephanie did, including her need to care for herself. She suffered from depression. When she moved to Brooklyn she started actively seeking treatment. For her, tending to her mental health was directly connected to her search for work. "I'm not gonna be in the frame of mind to work and be a good employee if my mindset is not correct." Stephanie framed her worries about both her weight gain and her mental health in terms of her ability to work. She saw these multiple health challenges primarily as an impediment to finding and keeping employment, reflecting David Harvey's observation that "illness under capitalism is defined as an inability to work"(Harvey 2000).

Dominic pursued day labor and side hustles while he looked for more permanent work. A month after they moved into the shelter, he finally landed a job as a janitor. Stephanie was relieved, but the reality of the low-wage labor market is that permanent employment with a single employer is becoming increasingly rare. The janitor job was a temporary full-time position, meaning Dominic was only hired for sixteen weeks. Once that was done, he would have to wait a certain amount of time before he could be reinstated in another assignment because the employer did not want to pay for unemployment or benefits. Stephanie hoped something good would come of it, but she wasn't optimistic. Moving in and out of marginal employment while trying to maintain access to the benefits her family needed, like food stamps, was a challenge and had serious health implications for the well-being of Stephanie and Dominic's family.

HEALTH IMPACT OF WORK-FIRST WELFARE

Stephanie's health had suffered along with her family's financial stability. Even in the short term, the health impact of Stephanie's situation was evident. She clearly saw her weight gain as an effect of both the stress of the past two years and the fact that she could only afford the cheapest food in the grocery store. She brought pictures to show me what she had looked like back when her family's financial situation had been more stable. Looking at the photos she said, "That is not the same person—over fifty pounds gained, even before the pregnancy. I was a little cutie, healthy, happy, vibrant. Now, physically, everything, it's terrible. This has just been too much to take."

Even with a full food stamp allotment, many un- or underemployed families still ration food. Food stamps are based on the USDA's thrifty food plan and were designed as a supplement to another form of income—either low wages or welfare benefits. The USDA has four food plans that the agency uses to make recommendations about food budgets for a range of circumstances— the thrifty food plan, the low-cost food plan, the moderate-cost plan, and the liberal plan. The thrifty food plan is the least expensive and "serves as a national standard for a nutritious diet at a minimal cost and is used as the basis for maximum food stamp allotments" (US Department of Agriculture 2007). It is devised by nutritionists who look at spending patterns, recommended daily allowances of all nutrients, and the average price of grocery items to come up with a recommended grocery basket that comes close to meeting nutritional needs on a minimal budget. The plan presumes a considerable departure from standard American eating patterns as well as considerable skill in budgeting, cooking, and knowledge about food.

In practice, the thrifty food plan is inadequate to meet most families' food needs. Studies have found that "about 80 percent of all benefits are used within the first 2 weeks of issuance, and more than 91 percent of all benefits are used by the 21st day. Evidence suggests the caloric intake of SNAP recipients declines 10 to 15 percent at the end of the month, and admissions to hospitals for hypoglycemia increase significantly among food insecure diabetics" (Institute of Medicine and National Research Council 2013). Stephanie was trying to feed a family of three on a food stamp budget for two over the course of six months—something that proved impossible to do. No amount of stretching could make up for the difference between what they received in benefits and their family's food needs. Trying to fill these gaps while Dominic was left off the case and then sanctioned created inordinate hardship for Stephanie and her family. They tried to shelter their son from the reality of their situation. As she put it, "He's like in a bubble. The only time he really feels it is when we have the food situation."

It is hard to hide hunger from children and these early experiences can have long-term health consequences. Exposure to adverse childhood experiences, including hunger, are strongly associated with higher prevalence of disease later in life, including diabetes, cardiovascular disease, and depression (Danese, Moffitt, and Harrington 2009). The stress of hunger and food insecurity weighs on people's bodies and minds, both in the short term and the long term. Though Stephanie tried to protect her son, there was no way to shield him from the fact that they could not afford food. "It's especially hard for my child. He's used to having that choice. 'Can I have grapes today?' I don't have that. What do I have to give him? I have to look. I have some saltine crackers. Maybe that'll do. So, he just says, 'Forget it.' Every time he says forget it. I hate it. He wants something. And I can't give it to him. And that's not fair."

The situation only got worse when Stephanie and Dominic moved into the shelter. Even though they had finally started receiving the full food stamp allotment for a family of three, they no longer had a kitchen where they could cook. The cooking facility in the shelter was in a common area and was run down. The stove was old and often didn't work. Stephanie didn't want to keep food in the shared refrigerators because it might go missing. Instead, she relied on the mini fridge and microwave in their single room, which meant she could only buy and store small quantities of food. Shopping this way is more expensive. She worried about how they would make do when they first moved. "We still ration at the end of the month with the $526 (the full food stamp allotment). So, could you imagine how we're going to pull it off not having cooking and eating out, eating prepared meals that are more expensive and all of that? I have no idea."

Over the next few months, Stephanie's health continued to deteriorate. She was plagued with chronic tooth infections and she was diagnosed with high blood pressure. "A lot of the stuff we've been eating is, you know what I mean, not the best stuff. Or we go out to eat, dollar menus here or there. Whatever. Take advantage of the lunch specials for dinner. You compensate with the prices. You try to work it out." Stephanie was well aware that eating this way was not healthy, but without secure, decently paid work there was very little she could do to improve her family's diet. No amount of stretching or budgeting could empower Stephanie and her family to eat better in a consumer market where the cheapest calories are also the unhealthiest. Like many un- and underemployed families, Stephanie and her family had *eating is political* (margin annotation)

to risk long-term health impacts in order to meet their short-term hunger.[1]

Stephanie's health problems, including her weight gain and high blood pressure, point to a complicated truth about food. Eating is always political and embodies a set of social relationships that can be based in power and domination or in care and commensality (Appadurai 1981). "Consumption is not a simple matter of self-replacement, then, but the recognition and monitoring of relationships" (Strathern 1988, 302) Stephanie's deteriorating health was an embodiment of her deteriorating economic citizenship status. Her family's ability to make claims on the state and on employers for basic subsistence, including for food that would support her family's health, was deeply compromised by a food safety net that prioritizes the responsibilities of citizens to be productive, employable, and submissive to the needs of the market above all else. At the same time, employers are free to abandon their commitments to providing well-paid or secure employment and the state takes little responsibility for ensuring either adequate employment or economic security.

Though the Bloomberg administration professed to consider food policy "primarily from a public health angle," the public implied here is increasingly narrow. Bloomberg did not imagine a broad public of citizens with equal rights to food and health. Instead, citizenship itself was defined as a set of responsibilities and obligations on the part of the poor. The primary responsibility was to work and to contribute to a city that was imagined as a business. In this framework, responsible citizens who were employed would be incentivized with SNAP benefits to buy better food while irresponsible citizens (those who don't work) could be abandoned by the state and left to rely on charity or to eat at the whim of the grocery store.

HEALTHY EATING AND EMERGENCY FOOD

Like many families, Stephanie found it necessary to turn to food pantries because SNAP and what she and her husband could earn from the temporary jobs they found fell short. Many conservatives have argued that these local, voluntary efforts are preferable to federal food programs, like SNAP because they "come from the heart." Congressional Republican Paul Ryan has vociferously attacked food stamps as "unsustainable" and "cold," sapping the initiative of both recipients and communities to do the good work of caring for the poor. At the same time, he has heaped praise on voluntary organizations like food pantries and soup kitchens. "We Americans give ourselves to every kind of good cause. We do so for the simple reason that our hearts and conscience have called us to work that needs doing.... A lot of good happens without government commanding it, directing it, or claiming credit for it. That's how life is supposed to work in a free country" (Ryan 2012).

Emergency food providers have long been criticized for having little to no regard for the health impact of the food they offer. Emergency food programs have historically embodied the old saying that beggars can't be choosers and have served primarily as dumping grounds for the leftovers of our industrial food system (Fitchen 1988; Poppendieck 1998; Lohnes and Wilson 2018). However, as diet-related diseases among the poor began to garner national attention, food banks and emergency food providers began putting public health at the center of their programming and missions. Efforts have been made to improve the food distributed at pantries and soup kitchens (Carney 2015). The North Brooklyn Pantry was no exception. They held a series of fundraising dinners to bring "healthy organic food to the people of

North Brooklyn" that were always well attended and raised thousands of dollars each year. They also participated in a grant funded program that brought fresh produce to the pantry from nearby upstate farms each week in the summer. The program provided a special volunteer, the veggie educator, who explained how to cook unfamiliar vegetables and encouraged pantry clients to try new foods. Despite these efforts, food pantries and soup kitchens struggle to offer adequate, healthy food, in part because, as charitable organizations, their own funding and resources are so inconsistent. Food pantries regularly have nothing or very little to offer and consistently report turning people away because of a lack of food (Koible and Stampas 2016).

Stephanie's deepest period of food crisis, trying to stretch a food stamp budget for a family of two, took place during the summer of 2011. That summer was a particularly bad time for pantries in New York City, marked by serious food shortages. I had been volunteering at the North Brooklyn Pantry for six months at that point and had not thought much about where the food was coming from. I wondered why we seemed to have more food than we could handle one week, and the next we would barely have enough. Some weeks we gave out full bags with peanut butter, bread, vegetables, frozen chicken, and pasta and the next week we would have cans of gravy, soup, bulk gummy drops that we had to bag and some past-date matzah. Word would get out in the neighborhood on days when we had a better selection, and the line outside the church would swell. If we ran out of a coveted item, like meat, complaints would ensue for the rest of the day. People talked and word traveled fast. Expectations were raised, and, more often than not, deflated when we ran out of preferred foods before the end of the day. But we always had enough food to be able to give out something to the

$15 a week
veggie
for 2

several hundred people who showed up each week. Toward the end of the day the bags might be a little lighter, but we almost never had to turn anyone away.

Then, one summer day, eight months after I began volunteering, we suddenly had almost no food to give out. The pantry closed early for several weeks that summer, turning away local residents who came every week to pick up food. The bags we did give out before we closed for the day were nearly empty. Christine, the veggie educator assigned to the North Brooklyn Pantry, handed out vegetables with the only other food we had that summer, hundreds of cans of corn. The fresh vegetables ran out quickly, but we had more corn than we knew what to do with. It was more than people wanted and more than we could give away. Katherine, one of the regular volunteers, described a typical interaction with a client during those weeks. "Yesterday this lady told me, all I get is corn? I told her, we're running low and all the Food Bank gave us was these cases of corn. If you don't want it, give it back to me. And she's still fussing. And I said, what do you want from me? Something's better than nothing"

It wasn't just the North Brooklyn Pantry. When the truck came with our delivery, all the pallets looked like ours—piles of canned corn. Renee, a director from another local pantry complained about running out of food. "We've since had some droughts where it's like 'would you like some corn?' I'm sure you've been through that. It was like, man cannot live on corn alone." Yolanda, the director of a large pantry in Williamsburg reported that, "It came a point that every week you would go into the [ordering] system it was like fifty cases of corn, but nothing else. Fifty cases. We were just bagging corn and we would tell them, this is all we have. And we had the HPNAP grant, so I would just order rice to go with their corn.[2] There was nothing else to do. We were giving them like four or five cans of corn."

Over the next year, as I met with other pantry directors from around the city and asked them where they got their food from, the conversation inevitably turned to "that corn." On a conference call about federal budget cuts with food pantry directors from across the city, a frantic director from Staten Island came on the line late. She apologized for missing the first few minutes of the call and then asked what was going on. "Did the cuts already happen? Our shelves are bare. All we have is corn."

Stephanie and others like her who relied heavily on food pantries and soup kitchens immediately felt these shortfalls. That summer, she frequented several pantries to get enough food to eat. Typically, people who are excluded from welfare protections are the most heavily reliant on food pantries, including immigrants who are excluded from SNAP if they are undocumented or if they are documented but have been in the United States for less than five years (Mares 2013). Because most pantries in New York City are getting the majority of their food from the same state-funded sources, this means the poorest people are the most hurt by these shortfalls. Stephanie was trying to cobble together enough food each month for her family. Like other families who relied heavily on food pantries, she often fell short. A single mother who frequented the North Brooklyn Pantry described her situation during the summer of corn: "Right now, it's really thin. There's less in your cupboard. At some point, you have nothing."

Over dinner one night, another regular at the North Brooklyn Pantry's soup kitchen observed, "I go to a couple other pantries and try to get stuff. But the food they give us is like yams and corn. It's the same food at every pantry. Like six years ago I was going to pantries and stuff and one place would have some meat, another place would have some vegetables. So, you'd hit two or three pantries, you'd have enough for like two or three days. And now it's like, nobody is donating anything other than corn and yams. How much do they think the poor want to eat corn and yams, you know? I'll eat a whole can of corn, when I know that's just not healthy for you. Your body doesn't digest corn like that, but I'll eat the whole can because I'm hungry."

His explanation for the food shortages, that all people want to donate is corn and yams, speaks to the general impression most people have that food from pantries comes from private donations. This pervasive but faulty notion is aided and abetted by political rhetoric that extols the virtues of charity for addressing hunger and scorns federal entitlements like SNAP that ensure Americans have access to food. However, emergency food providers are best understood as shadow state institutions (Gilmore 2009), brought into being by state funding streams that promote an illusion of a private, charitable sector distributing donated food.

The shortfall Stephanie and others faced during the summer of corn was not caused by a lack of private donations. It was caused by spending cuts at the USDA for programs that buy up surplus commodities that are then distributed through food banks, soup kitchens, and food pantries across the nation. There are two main streams of USDA funding for EFPs. The first is the mandatory funds that are earmarked by Congress for purchasing food. The other stream is discretionary funds that can fluctuate from year to year. The purpose of the discretionary funds is not to provide food to hungry families, but to support farmers when their crop prices fall. Commodity prices had been high in 2011, so farmers were selling their products on the market and needed less support from the USDA to remain profitable. The discretionary funding, which is basically intended as a market intervention when commodity prices are low, had typically made up about half of the TEFAP food that came to EFPs prior to 2011. But as commodity prices rose, and as pressure for austerity and spending restraint took hold in Washington, discretionary purchases of food dropped. These market dynamics were felt all across New York City that summer as food pantries turned hungry people away or handed them nothing but a can of corn.

The impact on families like Stephanie's was serious, but largely invisible. Food pantries are under no obligation to ensure that people have enough to eat. When they are unable to meet people's needs, because of budget cuts or increasing community needs, they simply turn people away at the door. Stephanie's family eats at the whim of the grocery store where she has to buy the cheapest foods in order to maximize quantity. But they also eat at the whim of the employers who choose to hire her or not, the welfare office workers who decide whether or not to apply sanctions to her family's case, and the policy makers who cut food stamp and TEFAP spending in order to balance budgets. Whether Stephanie and her family eat and what they eat is determined by an interlocking system of work, welfare, food policy, and consumer markets that determine who gets what. Her and her family's health hangs in the balance of these larger forces.

BODIES AS COMMODITIES

Despite the growth of the food safety net over the past twenty years, rates of food insecurity have remained virtually flat; obesity rates have continued to climb, as have rates of diet-related disease (Chilton and Rose 2009). The enormous growth in the food safety net has had virtually no impact on the levels of food insecurity, obesity or diet-related disease. As conditions of poverty, insecurity, and precarity worsen, the nutrition safety net is fraying at the edges, despite growing resources dedicated to the task of addressing people's nutritional needs. As Stephanie's experience shows, our current political commitment to a safety net built around work directly contributes to deteriorating public health as the conditions of work themselves deteriorate. Lauren Berlant calls this fraying of the body under capitalist regimes "slow death," which she defines as "the physical wearing out of a population and the deterioration of people in that population that is very nearly a defining condition of their experience and historical existence" (Berlant 2007).

Bloomberg's commitments to both work-first welfare and improving public health are rooted in an economistic perspective that views people primarily as commodities. Residents' health and well-being is valued so long as they are understood as workers. Policy makers and public health officials encourage the poor to maintain a work-ready body (and produce work-ready children) in both subtle and not-so-subtle ways. In this view, bodies are understood as productive property that must be tended to. Not tending to your body is a sign of neglect, not just at the personal level, but a neglect of your duty to be productive for the greater good—for the market. It is each individual's duty to invest in their own human capital. Obesity, then, is seen as a failure to consider one's own long-term economic viability. Citizens who are impacted by public health crises, like rising rates of diabetes, are seen as future economic liabilities in need of medical care and aid. As such, they require policy intervention to encourage or enforce better eating habits in order to reduce future cost burdens.

People like Stephanie struggle for inclusion in a city that actively works to exclude and expel those who are seen as the nonproductive poor. Bloomberg's commitment to work-first welfare policies actively excludes poor people from assistance, for example, by sanctioning welfare recipients for minor—even absurd—infractions like Dominic's failure to dress properly. The Bloomberg administration's policies were designed to make life difficult for the nonproductive poor, thereby encouraging them to leave the city. His administration instituted a program that cost half a million dollars annually to divert homeless families from the shelter system by paying for their travel costs out of the city (Bosman 2009). As one analyst of Bloomberg's legacy put it, "The mayor's subliminal message winnows down to this: 'Good luck and send us a postcard from Ohio'" (Bellafante 2013).

In an era of labor surplus, approaching the city like a business means shedding those citizens who are no longer needed. Our economy does not need all the workers who need work. Though the official unemployment rate has been falling steadily, the labor force participation rate—that is, the percentage of adults currently engaged in work—is at its lowest level since the 1970s. Technology is likely to make many more workers redundant in the coming decades (Ford 2015, Brynjolfsson and McAfee 2011). Stephanie and Dominic's experience of temporary, insecure work does not have a clear solution on the horizon, and many more people are likely to find themselves in the same boat. Many researchers and theorists have begun to wonder if we are facing a post-work future (Frase 2016). With our current welfare and food security policies, such a future would guarantee the continued existence of an underclass of Americans who struggle both economically and with poor health outcomes.

On the one hand, there are long-standing, deeply embedded ideas about poverty and work that are animating food stamp policy and welfare policy more generally. These neoliberal moves toward privatization and marketization shift resources toward poor people who earn wages and away from those who are left out of the labor force. This shift has an impact on how hunger manifests and is experienced by the urban poor. On the other hand, new discourses about health and well-being have emerged. Food is at the center of this new imaginary, positing that people need to take responsibility for their health through smart food choices. Public health concerns are producing new sets of actors and agents who are concerned with both poverty and health. These competing concerns—punitive, neoliberal poverty governance and new sets of actors advocating around the right to health collide in a host of contradictory and messy ways around food and food policy. The image of the self-actualizing, empowered consumer citizen is coming up against the limits of below-subsistence wages. The obesity epidemic is producing new, widespread concerns over the future of the American labor force—imagined as literally weighed down by a surfeit of encumbered, inefficient bodies.

The modern economy, built around flexible labor, requires new forms of productive consumption, from the consumption of education to the consumption of food both to replenish the body and to maintain it as viable capital in an ever-evolving capitalist economy. Though Bloomberg emphasized the need for healthy bodies, many of his policies including his welfare policies produced food insecurity and sickness. These sick bodies were treated with disdain and as a burden on the city. Though the language of workforce development is often deployed in relationship to anti-hunger programs, the reality is that many workers are not needed and their long-term health really isn't a concern, except insofar as poor health represents a cost to the abstract notion of the city or the nation.

Our fractured food safety net keeps millions of Americans on the edge of food insecurity and forces them to rely on the cheapest and unhealthiest foods in the market. The costs of our punitive system of food assistance are borne out by the poor, who disproportionately suffer from ill health related to diet and stress. The beneficiaries of this system are employers who can profit off of paying employees below-subsistence wages and have access to an increasingly desperate labor pool who will work under increasingly poor conditions. Our current food safety net allows employers to enjoy a free lunch at the expense of people like Stephanie, who are so desperate for work they will "take anything."

Addressing the interlocking issues of food insecurity, obesity, and diet-related disease among the poor would require a restoration of economic rights. Instead of viewing the poor as a dependent labor force that earns economic citizenship rights through productivity, we would have to see food and health as basic human rights that must be protected without conditions. A rights-based approach would require us to think about how markets have failed and to question if there are solutions that exist outside (or even in opposition to) markets. That is, how do we design policies in ways that protect people from the vicissitudes and failures of the market? It would require us to ask not what the poor can give or what they cost our economy, but what they are owed.

CHAPTER SEVEN

Ending Hunger, Addressing
the Crisis

Nigel, whom we met in chapter 1, was still living in transitional housing six months after he returned to the North Brooklyn Pantry. After leaving his job at the diner he took on a series of temporary jobs. He helped a local contractor renovate a basement apartment for a few weeks, occasionally picked up short-term gigs through a temp agency and volunteered at the pantry. He regularly ran out of cash and food. I helped him reapply for SNAP, but his case was complicated by his work situation. Over the course of six months, his case had been reopened, moved to a different welfare office, closed, and reopened again. As we navigated the Kafkaesque web of documents, trips to the welfare office, bureaucratic mismanagement, and neglect, Nigel struggled with prolonged periods of food insecurity. His housing situation was just as complex and insecure. His landlord was trying to evict all the residents in his single-room-occupancy building to convert it to high-end apartments. Nigel and the other tenants had been engaged in a drawn-out court battle that added to his sense of precarity.

Nigel is an unusually upbeat person. As he once put it, "I'm the eternal optimist. Even if we're going down in flames I can say, wow, what a cool flame we're going down in." But his circumstances were taking a toll on him. One winter afternoon, after several months of managing these various insecurities, he showed up at the pantry with a long face. I had never seen him so down. He told me about a dream he had the night before. He was stuck in a pit of thick mud. As he tried to pull himself out, he kept catching glimpses of opportunities literally passing him by. He was depressed about his inability to get his life back on track and he struggled to understand what had gone wrong. "The drive that once drove this engine, somewhere it went askew. It went off track. And when I went off track, instead of going to the body shop I found a crew of half-assed mechanics who just jerry-rigged the engine to just keep it going. And that's what's going on right now. I need to get into a Midas shop and get an overhaul. I need something to believe in." It was unclear what that something might be. The jobs he found all felt like dead ends. He considered going to culinary school or getting a nursing degree but was unsure how he would pay for it. All he was able to do was patch together the pieces of his life to keep going, but he was losing faith that he would ever be able to get back on track to a regular life, which for him meant having a steady job and an apartment of his own.

There was a sense that the stability he had known in the past was gone and getting back to where he wanted to be remained elusive. Whether this was the result of his own failures or something bigger than himself was an open question for Nigel. "When Obama got elected, I thought there was going to be a big peace corps revival of American society. Of course, I thought he was a magic Negro too. And it just wasn't so. I don't want to use some bizarre current society to break down why I'm in your office today. I don't want to say "Obama," but that was just the beginning of the popping of the balloon, and the air's been seeping ever since. I don't mean, I'm not trying to blame anything—there was just this big anticlimax. This huge build up and then, meh. I'm not blaming, I shouldn't have even brought his name into this story, but just the whole spirit of things. Something isn't there that used to be there. That's the underlying theme. Something is missing in the stew. And I think it's me. It needs more Nigel in the soup. And I don't know where that ingredient is anymore."

Like so many Americans facing real economic anxiety, Nigel did not have a clear sense of how to move forward. He had not yet given up on the idea that he could turn his situation around, maybe by working harder or finding the drive he felt he had when he was younger. Or maybe he could get more training and education and that would put him back on the path to stability. Maybe he could work harder and develop his human capital in ways that would pay off, lifting him out of his slump. He wondered if he could transform himself, by sheer will or through education, into a person who could once again attain what he saw as self-sufficiency. That is, he wondered if he could work his way back to a position in society that offered a modicum of security. The forces working to exclude him—from a profit-driven housing market that offered little protection, a costly education system, and work-first welfare policies that pushed him off the SNAP rolls—presented roadblocks at every turn (Seefeldt 2016). At the same time, he wanted something to believe in and imagined that, perhaps, there could be some broader transformation—a big peace corps–type revival of American society—that could go beyond the jerry-rigged fixes *good question*

that just kept things going. Nigel imagined, however tentatively, collective solutions to the problems he faced. What kind of politics would give people in his situation something to believe in? What would a big "peace corps revival" of American society look like?

These are questions that are rarely raised in the public sphere. Neoliberalism, some have argued, has entered its "zombie phase" (Peck, Theodore, and Brenner 2009). With no coherent alternatives, the projects of privatization, marketization, and exclusion proceed out of sheer inertia. Nigel understood the limits of Obama-era politics that seemed to promise but ultimately failed to provide new solutions for the deep, entrenched, economic transformations that have produced historic levels of inequality in the United States and around the world. His experience, trying to get back on his feet and finding nothing but pantry bags and dead-end jobs, illuminates the limits of the sclerotic neoliberal response to poverty. Nigel was grateful for the help he found. Without the hard work of organizations like the North Brooklyn Pantry, he would have much been worse off. Federal food assistance and emergency food providers play an important role in making sure that people can eat. But these institutions, as they are currently structured, are designed to manage poverty and food insecurity, not to end it.

Scholars who study food insecurity have long advocated for a rights-based approach to food in the United States and globally (Chilton and Rose 2009, Carney 2015, Messer and Cohen 2007). Guaranteeing a right to food, particularly in the United States where food is so abundant, is a simple technical problem and an enormously challenging political problem. In their groundbreaking work, Dreze and Sen point out that hunger and famine are not caused by food shortages, but by what they call entitlement failures (Dreze and Sen 1989). That is, people lack food because they cannot adequately make and enforce a claim to the food that exists. Nowhere is the relationship between food insecurity and entitlement failure more evident than in the United States, where food is so bountiful and overproduction and food waste are significant problems. Between 30 and 40 percent of the food produced in the United States is thrown away (US Department of Agriculture 2013). Yet people like Stephanie, whom we met in chapter 5, skip meals so that her child has food to eat. This paradox requires us to consider what James Ferguson calls the politics of distribution. "In a world of massive overproduction and widespread poverty, it seems almost embarrassingly obvious that what is needed most ... are better ways of making sure the abundant yield ... gets properly spread around to those who are, at present, not getting their share" (Ferguson 2015, 38).

In the US context, entitlement failure is bound up in the notion that work is and should be the primary mechanism for distributing goods and services. The right to food is tied to the obligation to work. As Michael Harrington put it, "St Paul's injunction—he who does not work shall not eat—is the basis of the political economy of the West" (Harrington 1962). Aside from the independently wealthy, the only legitimate way to get food is by working, depending on a worker, or claiming an inability to work because of old age or disability. US lawmakers have continually opposed enshrining a right to food in federal and international law precisely because doing so would require providing universal, unconditional food assistance regardless of employment status (Messer and Cohen 2007).

However, work has become an increasingly ineffective system for distributing basic goods and services in the latter half of the twentieth century (Standing 2011, Kalleberg 2011). The expansion of SNAP assistance, beginning in the early twenty-first century, is a political response to work as a failing system of distribution. Food assistance is emblematic of a new mode of post-Fordist poverty governance that is both exclusionary and inclusionary. As employers walk away from even basic obligations of the employment relationship like paying employees enough to afford rent and food, employees are offered work supports from the state to keep them afloat in an increasingly uncertain labor market. At the same time, people like Nigel who struggle to find stable work are routinely barred from assistance. Exclusion and inclusion work hand in hand to regulate growing social and economic marginality in the twenty-first century (Sassen 2014, Beckett and Western 2001, Hinton 2016).

The recent political upheavals in the United States and globally, marked by increased political polarization and the rise of far-right populism, suggest that perhaps we are hitting the limits of this form of governance. Despite relentlessly upbeat statistics about tight labor markets and a strong recovery from the Great Recession, eviction rates remain high (Desmond 2015), millions of people who want full-time work can only find part-time work (Bureau of Labor Statistics 2018) and the middle-wage jobs that were shed in the last economic downturn have largely been replaced by low-wage jobs (National Employment Law Project 2014). The sense of unease among the American electorate, despite an official economic recovery, has destabilized American politics. In this context, the experiences and perspectives of people who live on the edge of hunger are important because they can point us toward a more effective politics.

Ending food insecurity in the United States demands a new politics of inclusion. The experiences of food insecure families, their desires and analysis of their own situation is key to understanding what a new politics of inclusion might look like. In her groundbreaking ethnography on Black girlhood and citizenship, Aimee Meredith Cox challenges the "paternalistic politics of care that denies Black girls the right to live outside the market logic that sees them first and foremost as laborers in the service of everyone but themselves, as perpetually struggly [*sic*], and as bodies that need to be disciplined or reshaped to begin to approach legibility as worthy citizens" (Cox 2015, 118). She insists on shifting the focus of so much social science literature that frames Black youth as a problem to be solved. Instead, she asks what can be learned from young Black women about how institutions need to shift in ways that would have widespread social benefits. Following her lead, I ask, what can food-insecure people, struggling to feed themselves on the systemic edge of inclusion and exclusion tell us about the kinds of politics and claims to entitlement needed to ensure a right to food in the United States today? How would institutions need to shift to ensure a right to food to all the people in this book? What does food citizenship look like if we take food-insecure people's perspectives and experiences seriously? How do hungry people living in the United States articulate and act on a right to food? What kinds of inclusion do they want?

Ensuring a right to food requires a fundamental transformation of the link between food assistance and work. Again and again, the people I met at the North Brooklyn Pantry who struggled with food insecurity pointed to the failures of the labor market as the cause of their food troubles. When I asked what would allow them to eat the way they would like to, I almost inevitably heard "a job that pays," "being financially stable." And yet, no one thought simply attaining a job was a path out of poverty. Jobs that pay too little, are temporary, or don't allow flexibility for childcare were seen as obstacles in their own right. In fact, for many people resistance to exploitative work or work conditions was often a precursor to increased food insecurity.

Nigel and Jimmy quit their jobs when they were asked to take less than minimum wage, pushing them both into prolonged periods of crisis and food insecurity. Adwa resisted what she saw as exploitative work that did not provide her the time or resources she needed to care for her children. Fabiola rejected work in the formal labor market, choosing instead to treat her volunteer work as a job that gave her the flexibility and freedom she wanted. Despite her hunger and her poverty, she consistently refused working in a job that she saw as leading nowhere while taking a toll on her body and her life. Like Nigel and Adwa, she was opposed to the conditions of the work that was available to her. People like Adwa, Jimmy, and Stephanie who struggle with food insecurity were sharply critical of the growing informality, insecurity, and low pay they encountered in the labor market. They were extraordinarily clear on the conditions that caused food insecurity and the measures necessary to end it.

Taking hungry people's resistance as a guide, I suggest several institutional shifts that would improve the systems of distribution in the United States to ensure that all people have access to adequate food. Some of these suggestions go well beyond the narrow confines of the food safety net and do not represent minor policy changes to the current system of food assistance. There are, of course, important reforms, like increasing SNAP benefit amounts or getting rid of SNAP work requirements, that would significantly improve food access and reduce food insecurity (Gunderson, Kreider, and Pepper 2018; Ziliak 2016). But food insecurity is, ultimately, a symptom of poverty. Broadly addressing poverty will require a much broader politics than instituting minor policy changes to food assistance programs. In order to be effective, this broader politics will have to speak to the aspirations of a wide swath of the American public, including those who are socially and economically marginalized. These proposals are not grounded in or constrained by what is currently politically possible but are intended to disrupt the current reformist approach to questions of poverty and food insecurity. The ideas below are driven by the analysis and insights of hungry people themselves.

REIMAGINING A RIGHT TO FOOD

Asserting that all people have a right to food raises a host of complicated political, economic, and ethical considerations. What kind of claims can people make to the things they need and how can they enforce those claims? For Fabiola, the answer to this question was a simple one. "Being hungry is not based on how much money you make. It's the fact that you don't have resources to be able to buy food and feed your stomach. That's how I feel.... Rent is astronomical. You can pay $1000-plus, and those people struggle. Why shouldn't they be entitled to get food? They say they don't want to take, but OK, tell me what you have to eat right now. If you don't have anything, this is here for you. It's fine. As a matter of fact, take from what I have here, because if you tell me you don't have it—I am OK with that. Because of the fact that I need food, it shouldn't matter how much money I make. It shouldn't matter if I make $600 a week or $50 a week."

Fabiola recognized the demands of people in need as valid and binding. From her perspective, "If I tell you I need food, I need food, and I shouldn't have to bring to you a list of documents. It shouldn't be that way." She did not see the right to food as contingent on reciprocity in the form of work for wages, proper behavior, or even any particular measure of poverty. For her, the food we handed out at the pantry was a form of collective wealth that everyone had a right to, regardless of income or work status. Her perspective of food as a commonly held community resource from which everyone can demand a share is certainly not unprecedented. Anthropologists have noted a range of societies in which food sharing is culturally enforced through the demands people make to their "rightful share" of the resources in the community (Lee 1979, Woodburn 1998, Ferguson 2015). Fabiola did not see food as something that must be earned but as something that must be equitably distributed. Distributing food was not an act of generosity or kindness but an effort to ensure that everyone was getting their fair share.

The belief that food should be shared and that all people have a right to eat is a deeply human impulse. Today this impulse is largely captured and expressed through the extensive network of emergency food providers in the United States. It takes the form of charity, tinged by sympathy and pity. Emergency food providers are understood broadly as providing food to people in need as a gift or as an act of generosity, not as fulfilling a right to food. Pantry directors and advocates who are engaged directly in emergency food are often intensely aware of the limits of charity. In a speech at an Annual Food Bank Conference, which gathers together pantry staff and volunteers from across New York City, Tony Butler, the director of the largest food pantry in Brooklyn, exhorted; "We can mask the justice issue because we're caught up with the charity. We mask it by thinking we— us in this room—can solve the hunger issue. We can't. We are just responding to it. The whole social structure has to respond to this hunger problem." Anti-hunger advocates and volunteers like Fabiola struggle to ensure a right to a fair share of food under a system that is designed to ensure scarcity and enforce charity.

Fabiola's approach to food poses a serious challenge to the underpinnings of the current food safety net. Not only does she assert an absolute right to food and an obligation to distribute food to those without the means to pay for it, she insists on decoupling the right to food from the obligation to work and from ideas of charity. Currently, her approach is hampered by the shortfalls and insufficiency that effect pantries and soup kitchens in New York and across the United States. Though her intention was to make sure people who needed food got food, in practice we often gave people far less than they needed and, in some cases, turned people away when we ran out of food. As we saw in chapters 5 and 6, the insufficiency of food pantries is a direct result of their structure as public/private partnerships designed to do more with less.

However, food distribution programs and community meal programs do not inherently undermine the right to food. With sufficient state funding and a political commitment to ending hunger, food distribution programs and soup kitchens have the potential to effectively improve universal access to sufficient food. State-funded communal kitchens and food distribution programs in Latin America offer alternative models of providing food to local communities that are less stigmatizing and more empowering than the charitable model that has taken root in the United States (Chappell 2018, Fernandes 2007). Social movements have often incorporated communal meal preparation and food distribution programs that address the needs of poor communities in ways that empower local residents and build solidarity across lines of difference (Nelson 2012, Dickinson 2013). These projects offer insight into how emergency food providers could be transformed as part of a broader commitment to establishing a right to food. It is possible to reframe charitable food as a community resource, designed to meet the needs of a diverse range of community residents, including rent-burdened families and overworked parents. Doing so would require significant resources from the state to ensure that pantries and soup kitchens can more fully meet the needs of a range of residents in their communities.

In the United States, the charitable approach of emergency food providers is often contrasted with the rights-based approach embodied by SNAP (Poppendieck 1998). Though SNAP does provide legal mechanisms through which people can assert their right to assistance, it is also structured in ways that enforce scarcity. In practice, Fabiola's approach to food assistance would ask us to do away with SNAP restrictions—those based on both work status and income—to ensure that all people who need food can be assured access. She also poses a challenge to the idea of food assistance as supplementary. SNAP is designed to supplement some other form of income—whether that is low wages or welfare benefits. On its own, SNAP does not provide enough food to ensure that people have enough to eat. Though SNAP does reduce food insecurity, the majority of SNAP households are still food insecure (Gunderson et al. 2018). Today, SNAP benefits most often supplement low wages and food from pantries and soup kitchens. Taking Fabiola's perspective to its logical conclusion would require changes to the program that would raise benefit levels so that the program is no longer supplementary but provides a rightful share. Expanding

SNAP as a universal entitlement to all residents in need would establish the program as a universal floor below which no one can fall, similar to calls for a universal basic income that would provide all residents in the United States with a guaranteed minimum income.

Like a universal basic income, increased SNAP benefits with no restrictions could go a long way toward guaranteeing a universal right to food and could eliminate hunger in the United States. However, like most universal basic income proposals, guaranteeing a right to food would not provide enough resources to resolve the broader issues of poverty. Ensuring a right to food through the expansion of emergency food providers as community kitchens or SNAP as a universal entitlement to adequate food would do very little to challenge the low wages and insecure work that are the root causes of so much food insecurity. While Fabiola resisted work in the formal economy, many of the other people at the North Brooklyn Pantry both wanted and needed a job.

DEMANDING A RIGHT TO WORK

Addressing the poverty and hunger caused by involuntary un- and underemployment as well as the poverty experienced by the working poor demands a dramatic shift in the way the labor market is regulated. Nigel hints at one possibility when he imagines a "big peace corps revival" of the United States. What he expected in the wake of Obama's election was an expansion of jobs with the express purpose of improving the nation and providing decent work to the people who needed it. What he and others like Jimmy and Stephanie wanted and needed was a regular job that paid enough to afford basic necessities and an apartment on their own. What they found when they sought assistance was a welfare system designed to push poor people off of the rolls and into a job with little regard for the quality of that employment.

Pushing people receiving assistance into low-wage work was the explicit policy under Mayor Bloomberg's administration. According to New York City's deputy commissioner of employment and contracts, enforcing work requirements for SNAP was intended "to get (recipients) motivated to find something better. It is to do soft skills. Get them working with others, get them thinking about if I'm making $10 an hour at a job, then I won't be so poor."[1] Subjecting people to work requirements is meant to motivate them by making the conditions of assistance so degrading and threadbare that even the worst job at the lowest wages is a preferable alternative (Piven and Cloward 1993). Workfare is designed to produce demoralized, desperate workers who will take any job, regardless of the conditions.

An inclusive politics that speaks to the needs and desires of people like Nigel, Stephanie, and Jimmy would flip work requirements on their head by offering people who seek assistance an opportunity to work at well-paid jobs that raise labor standards rather than lower them. Nigel's hope for a big peace corps revival in the United States reflects calls for a federal jobs guarantee that would offer well-paid work for everyone who wanted a job in the United States "through large-scale direct hiring by the federal government" (Paul, Darity, and Hamilton 2018). Rather than force applicants into substandard workfare jobs that pay below minimum wage and compensate people largely in food assistance, a federal jobs guarantee would provide well-paid work for people who need it. Arguments for a federal work guarantee build directly off of the idea, so foundational to the current welfare configuration, that work should be a path out of poverty—but acknowledge that this is currently not the case.

Calls for a job guarantee have a long history in the United States, rooted in struggles for both racial and economic justice. Franklin Roosevelt introduced the idea of a right to employment in his 1944 state of the union address (Paul et al. 2018). In the 1970s, Coretta Scott King spearheaded the National Committee for Full Employment/Full Employment Action Council, which lobbied for legislation that would guarantee employment for "all people who wanted jobs—where they were located, and at appropriate wages" (Stein 2016, 81). She argued that if the private market failed to provide jobs at a living wage then it was the responsibility of the federal government to step in and ensure people have access to well-paid work. These efforts grew out of her long-standing commitments to what she saw as the intertwined issues of racial justice, economic justice, and nonviolence. For her, there could be no true racial justice without an equal commitment to ensuring the economic rights of all people, and she saw full employment as one important way to achieve these interlocking goals (Stein 2016). Several prominent national policy makers, including 2020 presidential candidates Senator Cory Booker and Senator Bernie Sanders, have recently put forth proposals for various versions of a federal jobs guarantee based on the work of economists Pavlina Tcherneva, Darrick Hamilton, William Darity and Mark Paul (Paul et al. 2018, Tcherneva 2018). The Congressional Green New Deal resolution also includes a commitment to a federal jobs guarantee.

A federal jobs guarantee would alleviate a great deal of the hunger and food insecurity experienced by people at the North Brooklyn Pantry. Two of the primary drivers of food insecurity were involuntary unemployment and work that did not pay enough to afford basic necessities. By offering living-wage employment sufficient to afford basic necessities like food and rent, Nigel, Jimmy, Jesús, and Stephanie would not be left spending several years trying to dig themselves out of economic uncertainty. Instead of using hunger or the threat of hunger as a tool to prod people to accept low-paid, insecure work, we could expand the right to food by expanding the right to decently paid work and reestablishing full employment as a government mandate. Establishing a right to a job fundamentally alters work as a system of distribution by ensuring that all people who want to work have access to a job and, therefore, have access to a wage that can sustain them.

It also opens up the possibility of establishing the kinds of public institutions that could address so many of the food issues faced by people living in the United States today. One of the arguments against a federal jobs guarantee is that there will not be enough for people to do or that it will require the invention of thousands of meaningless or make-work jobs. But the efforts of food justice activists and anti-hunger advocates to transform the food system provide numerous projects that, if they were well staffed, would have tremendous positive impacts on the US food system. Emergency food providers tell us something very important about current US society. There are thousands of Americans willing to do an enormous amount of work to ensure that people have enough to eat and there is an acute need for these services. Urban agriculture, gardening programs, and food justice initiatives operate on shoestring budgets to expand access to healthy, sustainable food sources in urban settings subject to decades of racist disinvestment and abandonment (White 2011, Reese 2018). State led initiatives to address food insecurity in Brazil suggest several opportunities for putting people to work in the food system, from running publicly subsidized restaurants and improving school food programs to supporting small, rural producers through direct marketing programs to urban consumers (Rocha and Lessa 2010, Chappell 2018). Emergency food providers are already an unofficial employer of last resort for many un- and underemployed people like Fabiola, Angela, and Nigel who turned to volunteering as an economic survival strategy. Converting these volunteer positions into federally funded living-wage jobs would transform their precarious volunteer labor into stable employment and help to establish the kinds of institutions that could more effectively address food insecurity.

ADDRESSING THE CRISIS OF CARE

What gets defined as work is deeply political and has an enormous impact on who experiences food insecurity. In the United States, single mothers experience food insecurity at higher rates than any other demographic (Coleman-Jensen et al. 2017). The kinds of caring labor that people are expected to do has an impact on their ability to engage in paid employment. Recent studies have shown that motherhood has the biggest detrimental impact on earnings (Budig 2014). Mothers like Adwa were well aware that their caring labor was in direct conflict with their ability to financially support children. Adwa saw her situation as an impossible bind. She was expected to care for her children properly, and to do so by going to work. Yet the work she had access to was incompatible with her caring duties.

Adwa wanted a flexible schedule where she could take time off and be at home with her children and still be able to earn enough to care for them. She saw this labor as socially necessary and interdependent with the future needs of employers. "[Business owners] need to accommodate mothers' schedules. They need to know that, OK, we need you. And you need us. We need to work on the schedule. They need to be flexible. Without the next generation there are no people to continue [their business]. So, we need those people." She felt employers treated her as if the work she was doing to raise her children was a nuisance to their immediate needs. But Adwa saw things differently. She put it bluntly, "If you don't give birth, they say oh what happened? You are young, you are healthy why don't you give birth? What happened? Have children. And when you have them, they cause you problems. Oh, why do you have children? You want to depend on welfare. You want to depend on this service. We need a population, so why are you blaming me when I have them? They are talking like [these children] are not necessary. We need them later."

Adwa saw the need to expand the notion of work to include socially necessary care. Echoing the analysis of Marxist feminists, she insisted that private employers should provide flexibility in the form of paid time off, higher wages, more flexible schedules, and paid parental leave to absorb the costs of social reproduction (Bhattacharya 2013). At the same time, if employers were unwilling to accommodate mothers, then women should not be punished or stigmatized for receiving assistance from the state to care for their children. The blame and condescension Adwa felt from the welfare office workers made her feel like she was doing something wrong by seeking assistance. But she saw caring for her children as socially necessary labor that ought to be supported.

Adwa's demand that either employers should accommodate mothers or the state should offer support for caring work resonates with a long history of feminist organizing. Historically, women have targeted the state, insisting that caring for children is a job that should be valued and remunerated (Nadasen 2004). In the twenty-first century, childcare, food preparation, care of the sick and elderly, and cleaning services are growing employment sectors, raising questions about who is compensated for this labor and under what conditions. As Kathi Weeks points out, feminist activists who insisted on being paid for the caring labor they performed in their own households, like the wages for housework movement and the National Welfare Rights Organization "demystify the wage system insofar as (this demand) can draw attention to the arbitrariness by which contributions to social production are or are not assigned a wage" (Weeks 2011, 129). Adwa, who was paid for her work cleaning other people's houses, was punished with welfare sanctions when she insisted on her right to perform caring labor in her own home for her own children.

Expanding the right to jobs has to work hand in hand with expanding the idea of what counts as work. The socially necessary labor that Adwa identifies constitutes an unpaid second shift on top of the paid labor she is expected to perform. Establishing a federal right to a job has the potential to address Adwa's concerns in two ways. The first is that, in addition to non-poverty wages and benefits, a federal jobs guarantee could raise labor standards by providing flexibility and accommodations for caring labor. The second is that a federal jobs guarantee could expand public resources for social reproduction by supplying affordable child care, elder care and other public services like communal food preparation that would alleviate the care burden endured by so many women like Adwa.

Ending hunger in the United States requires a radical reorientation of the politics of distribution. We have more than enough food in the United States to ensure that everyone has access to healthy, sufficient food. What we do not have are systems in place to equitably distribute the food that exists. The seeds of a more equitable system of distribution are embedded within our current work- and charity-based approach. Though many of the proposals outlined here seem like a radical departure from our current safety net policies, they build off of the deep cultural attachment to work, community involvement, and the belief that all people have a right to adequate food.

In the unstable political present, the "thinkable" politics of supporting low wages through wage subsidies as a solution to poverty and hunger has run its course (Elwood and Lawson 2018). Expanding SNAP so that it once again operates as a floor under wages or establishing a right to well-paid work that can accommodate the needs of working caregivers may seem politically impossible. Indeed, these ideas would have been ridiculed as unthinkable just a few short years ago (and might still be today). But in the wake of social movements that have brought economic inequality, insecurity, and ongoing racial discrimination out into the national consciousness, including Occupy Wall Street, the Fight for 15, and Black Lives Matter, the terrain of what is politically thinkable has shifted. Several states and cities have enacted a $15-an-hour minimum wage—a demand that was considered absurd when fast food workers first walked off the job in 2011.

The reason why we have hungry people in the United States is because the right to food is tied to an obligation to work in an era where work is failing as a system of distribution for too many Americans. Changing the story requires understanding the cultural values people hold dear and around which they can be mobilized. We need new ideas that make the unthinkable politics of yesterday seem inevitable, so when the next crisis hits, the programs that get put in place transform the politics of hunger, either by changing work as a system of distribution or by breaking with it completely.

Postscript: The Right to Food in the Trump Era

The 2016 presidential election, along with the election of a majority of Republicans in both houses of Congress, posed a serious challenge to the food safety net in the United States. The Trump administration and Congressional Republicans have expressed open hostility to programs like SNAP and other safety net programs targeted to low-income households. However, both major political parties in the United States have been unwilling to address the broader politics of work and distribution in any meaningful way. Current debates over food assistance vacillate between drastically reducing access to assistance and maintaining the status quo described in this book. Congressional Republicans are currently trying to accelerate what in the past was a bipartisan agenda on work and welfare by introducing or tightening work requirements to SNAP, Medicaid, and housing assistance. In budget negotiations over the past several years, House Republicans have put forth proposals that cut SNAP by $80 billion to $150 billion over the next decade. The majority of these spending cuts come from tightening work requirements nationally. In a labor market where work is informalized and becoming harder to prove, tougher work requirements will make it likely that more people will lose access to benefits if they cannot show they are working (Philips 2016).

These proposals are explicitly modelled on the "success" of welfare reform. Success, in this case, is measured by the reduction in the welfare rolls, meaning reforms were successful largely because fewer people were able to access help.[1] According to the Center on Budget and Policy Priorities, prior to welfare reform 68 percent of families with children below the poverty line received assistance. Today only 23 percent do. In states like Louisiana and Texas only 4 percent of families in poverty have access to cash assistance (Pavetti 2016). Researchers have tied the significant rise in the number of people living in extreme poverty, defined as living on $2 a day or less, in the United States to the passage of welfare reforms that restricted access to cash for poor families (Edin and Shaefer 2016). The World Bank found that 3.2 million Americans lived on less than $1.90 a day in 2013 (Deaton 2018). These trends are likely to worsen if similar policies are enacted to restrict various forms of assistance, including SNAP. It is likely that we could see a return to the kind of hunger and malnutrition that spurred the expansion of the federal food stamp program in the 1970s.

While President Obama consistently vowed to veto cuts to SNAP, the Trump administration has signaled that it is willing to go even further than Congressional Republicans in restricting eligibility and spending on food assistance. The Trump administration's proposal to transform SNAP benefits from electronic benefits that can be spent like cash at the grocery store to a "harvest box" of predetermined, shelf-stable food items represents what I call the food pantry-fication of the

[handwritten margin note: denial of cultural needs.]

SNAP program. Instead of allowing low-income families to shop in stores like other consumers, they would have to take whatever foods were given to them, reproducing the same problems we have seen in pantries for decades (Poppendieck 1998). People with dietary needs, allergies, and restrictions would lose the ability to purchase the foods that meet their health needs. Further, this proposal would rob low-income people of their right to choose culturally appropriate foods. Though this proposal has been almost universally dismissed as impractical, it was an attempt to reset the terms of the debate over food assistance. In light of Trump's harvest box proposal, tightening work requirements and block granting SNAP seemed much more reasonable, despite the fact that these changes would spell disaster for the program's ability to respond to hunger and food insecurity.

Just as troubling is the Trump administration's proposed changes to the public charge rule under current immigration law. Historically immigrants could be denied visas or citizenship if they are found likely to become a "public charge," or a person who will be fully dependent on cash assistance or need long-term medical care at the government's expense. The Trump administration's proposal would expand the definition of a public charge to include programs like SNAP and public health insurance that legal permanent residents are currently entitled to. Legal permanent residents who qualify for these benefits would risk their ability to become citizens in the future if they apply for them or if they have used them in the past. It is unclear how this proposed rule would be administered, but it is already spreading fear in immigrant communities and forcing many families to choose between food and health assistance and their future citizenship status. However, the real goal of the proposed rule change is to inflame racial tensions and anti-immigrant sentiment by feeding the stereotype that immigrants unfairly benefit from programs paid for with tax payer money. Of course, this perspective ignores the fact that immigrants are tax payers who pay in far more than they receive in public benefits and that they are workers who are subject to the same poor labor conditions as US-born residents.

Adding or tightening work requirements to public assistance programs and denying citizenship to immigrants who access assistance both represent a deepening of exclusionary politics in the Trump era. These exclusions are not new, but the racist underpinnings of these policies are being made much more explicit than they were under previous administrations. Race and racism have long operated in the United States as a social and ideological means to create distinctions within the working class, dividing workers into groups who had access to the social wage and groups who did not (Katznelson 2005, Piven and Cloward 1993, Fox 2012). Immigration status continues to provide a legal avenue for producing a highly exploitable pool of low-wage labor. But in the wake of the civil rights struggles, which dismantled Jim Crow and ended legal discrimination, racial exclusions have taken on new forms. In the post–civil rights era, the expansion of prisons, policing, and punitive welfare regimes have become the coded ways that exclusionary racial regimes have been maintained (Alexander 2010; Haney-Lopez 2014; Soss, Fording, and Schram 2011). The view that SNAP must be made more restrictive in order to push undeserving freeloaders off the rolls is a direct extension of the racist attacks on cash assistance in the 1990s. The Trump administration's public charge rule builds off of this history by rhetorically painting immigrants as a racialized group that deserves to be excluded from help. Though the expanded work requirements proposed by House Republicans did not make it into the final 2018 Farm Bill, the USDA circulated a proposed rule change immediately after the bill was passed that would tighten work requirements by executive order. The anti-immigrant public charge rule is also moving forward through executive action as a means to drum up political support for the Trump administration. Unlike the political climate of the mid-1990s, the view that the food stamp program needs to be cut back remains deeply contested. The food stamp program remains enormously popular and most Americans oppose large cuts to the program (Delaney and Swanson 2013, Clement 2017).

Both anti-hunger advocates and Democratic policy makers have spoken out against the public charge rule and any new work restrictions, but they have been hesitant to directly address work as the basis of deservingness. Anti-hunger advocates point to how many SNAP recipients do, in fact, work and that the vast majority of SNAP recipients who do not work are children, disabled, or elderly and therefore exempt from the expectations that they can and should be employed. While they are opposed to deepening work requirements, they have taken a wholly defensive position, pushing for the Senate version of the Farm Bill that preserves the work requirements that are already there. Democrats have tried to sidestep the issue of work by reframing SNAP as a public health program. They argue that SNAP is an important nutrition program that allows people to eat better and maintain better health in the long run, so that they won't become future burdens on the state. Proposals to increase food stamp benefit amounts and to incentivize the purchase of fruits and vegetables with SNAP benefits in the 2014 farm bill negotiations represent an approach to food aid grounded in ideas of longer-term investment in human capital and public health. Raising benefit levels would significantly reduce levels of food insecurity in the United States (Gunderson, Kreider, and Pepper 2018).

However, emphasizing nutrition assistance and the protection of health to produce a productive labor force does very little to challenge work as the basis of deservingness. Hunger and ill-health become facts that are being addressed through the expansion of food aid—but questions about the kinds of structural violence that cause hunger and ill health are ignored. Nigel, Adwa, Jimmy, Fabiola, and Stephanie were far less concerned with food insecurity than they were with the conditions that produced food insecurity in the first place. For them, their tenuous, unstable relationship to the labor market made it difficult to claim a right to food. Anti-hunger advocates have been timid in challenging work requirements directly. As one high-level lobbyist told me, "We don't do very well on the work thing." Policy makers have been even more timid, choosing to focus on defending the work-based safety net, proposing increased funding for workfare programs, and encouraging healthy eating rather than on challenging the orthodoxy that assistance should be tied to work in the first place.

The politics of food in the United States are hotly contested and the tension between these two tendencies—doubling down on work enforcement and defending the food safety net as it is—has produced an unstable stalemate, with widespread hunger hanging in the balance. The increasingly authoritarian right wing has proposed making food policy more restrictive and bringing it further in line with welfare reforms that marginalize and punish the poor, tendencies that were well established in New York City under Mayor Bloomberg. At the same time, public health officials and anti-hunger organizations have successfully held off many of these efforts by tapping into a broadly circulating understanding of food and health and by touting the fact that so many food stamp recipients do, in fact, work. While Republican proposals will increase food insecurity and the hardships faced by poor people, the hard truth is that simply defending the status quo will not resolve the challenges faced by people in this book.

Defending the status quo is a losing strategy and a fundamental misread of the current political moment. It is time for Democrats to admit that welfare reform was a mistake. We cannot fix poverty by pushing people into a broken labor market and subsidizing their wages with tax credits and food stamps. There is no amount of job training or work enforcement that will magically create good jobs for all the people who have been left behind in our economy. We need to build new political alignments around the right to decent work, livable wages, and social protections. We need a new political common sense that taps into the deep dissatisfaction American workers have with stagnating wages and insecure benefits. The real threat in the current political moment is not that Republicans will succeed in pushing through this new round of welfare reforms and restrictions, but that no alternative will emerge to challenge the hegemony that poor people are to blame for their own poverty. Anti-immigrant sentiment and naked appeals to white nationalism will continue to flourish in the absence of political alternatives that speak to the real needs and desires of the working class. That is why the push for policies like a federal jobs guarantee are so important. The only way to establish a right to food in the United States is to change the terms of the debate.

solution

NOTES

CHAPTER ONE. FEEDING THE CRISIS

1. All names have been changed to protect the anonymity of the people who took part in this research. I have also changed the name of the food pantry where this research took place. The names of public officials in New York City who work on food and welfare policy have not been changed.

2. The food stamp program was renamed the Supplemental Nutrition Assistance Program (SNAP), as part of the 2008 stimulus bill. I use these terms interchangeably throughout the book because most people outside of government agencies and advocacy groups still refer to the program as food stamps.

3. Understanding how non-work operates as a racializing discourse demands a clear understanding of what race and racism are. Dorothy Roberts defines race as "a political category that has been disguised as a biological one" that "governs people by sorting them into social groupings based on invented biological demarcations." Racialization is a process through which particular groups are defined as inferior and therefore exploitable or disposable under capitalism. In this way, Ruth Wilson Gilmore explains that racism functions as "the state sanctioned or extralegal production and exploitation of group-differentiated vulnerability

to premature death." The work/non-work distinction operates as a racializing discourse and set of practices precisely because it builds off of and reinscribes preexisting racist ideas that African Americans possessed a "culture of dependency," marked by a lack of work ethic, thereby justifying cuts to welfare programs to encourage work.

4. The literature on the relationship between SNAP, obesity, and public health is too large to fully represent here. This research has mainly been carried out by medical researchers, nutritionists, and economists who have made contributions to the debates over how to restructure the program to incentivize healthy eating.

5. North Brooklyn is a predominantly white neighborhood. According to US census data, North Brooklyn is 64 percent non-Hispanic white, while the United States as a whole is 62 percent non-Hispanic white. According to the USDA, 43 percent of SNAP participants are white, 33 percent are African American, 19 percent are Hispanic, 2 percent are Asian, and 2 percent are Native American. Approximately 15 percent of the total US population currently receives SNAP. Though politicians on the right have attempted to use anti-Black racism to build support for cuts to the program, the image of hunger and SNAP use remains relatively free from the kind of racialized stereotyping that fueled welfare restructuring in the 1990s.

CHAPTER TWO. CARE AND ABANDONMENT IN THE FOOD SAFETY NET

1. Raj Patel writes, "In a Senate hearing George McGovern asked the school lunch program administrator, Rodney Leonard, if the Panthers fed more poor children than did the state of California.... Leonard admitted that it was probably true."

CHAPTER THREE. THE CARROT AND THE STICK

Parts of the argument in this chapter first appeared in my article "Working for Food Stamps: Economic Citizenship and the Post-Fordist Welfare State in New York City," *American Ethnologist* 43, no. 2 (2016): 270–81, 2016.

1. Research by James Ziliak notes that "the growth has been most rapid among full-time, full-year workers, as well as part-time, full-year workers," that is among households where at least one person is reliably employed. He also found that SNAP recipients are more educated today than they were thirty years ago. "The fraction of SNAP households headed by a high school drop out has plummeted by more than half to under 30 percent since 1980, and by 2011 more than a third of SNAP households were headed by someone with a college degree or more." (Ziliak 2016).

2. Though Adwa wanted to go to school and get an associate's degree, she was not offered any opportunity to count education for part of her work requirements. During the Bloomberg Administration this was standard practice in New York State, where fewer than 14 percent of welfare recipients were allowed to count school toward their work participation, despite the fact that federal law allows for up to 30 percent of the case load to be engaged in educational activities. Under the de Blasio administration, more welfare recipients have been able to count school as part of their work requirements (Dunlea 2009).

3. In December 2018 the issue of security guards at New York City's welfare offices calling law enforcement on clients garnered national attention when a video of police officers forcibly taking a child from a mother went viral. A *New York Times* article in response to the incident reported that between January 2017 and December 2018 "law enforcement agencies have been called to food-stamp offices across the city 2,212 times and have arrested 97 people, mainly for assault and offenses against public administration." These numbers reflect the many reports I heard from food pantry clients who reported being warned by welfare office workers that they would call security or who witnessed other clients being forcibly escorted out of the welfare office by security guards. Often the threats to call security were provoked by simple expressions of frustration on the part of clients.

CHAPTER FOUR. MEN, FOOD ASSISTANCE, AND CARING LABOR

1. The practice of profiting off of drug treatment programs is not isolated to this particular landlord or even to New York City. For an

in-depth of examination of the practice in Philadelphia, see Lubrano (2017).

2. I emphasize men's networks rather than simply using the term *family* to capture the range of reciprocal relationships men might be a part of. In the United States, the idea of family is commonly understood to mean a middle-class, privatized nuclear family comprised of a heterosexual couple and their children. Public policy has played a significant role in constructing this family form as the norm. However, anthropologists and others have long demonstrated that this narrow definition of family does not capture the multitude of supportive and reciprocal arrangements that exist, particularly in low-income communities in the United States. Carol Stack's classic work *All Our Kin* (1974) shows how reciprocal, familial networks of support can span several households and include "fictive kin" who may not count as or be recognized as "family" under dominant American ideas of kinship or state-enforced definitions of family.

3. According to the Joint Center for Housing Studies at Harvard University, "Cost burdens remain nearly universal among lowest-income households (earning under $15,000). Among this group, 83 percent were burdened in 2014, including 70 percent with severe burdens, paying more than 50 percent of their income for housing. Moderate-income households are also burdened by high housing costs. In the 10 highest-cost metros, three-quarters of renter households earning $30,000–$44,999 and half of those earning $45,000–$74,999 were cost burdened in 2014." (Joint Center for Housing Studies 2016, 4).

CHAPTER FIVE. FREE TO SERVE? EMERGENCY
FOOD AND VOLUNTEER LABOR

A version of this chapter first appeared as "Free to Serve: Emergency Food and Volunteer Labor in the Urban U.S.," *Gastronomica: The Journal of Critical Food Studies* 17, no. 2 (2017) 16–25.

1. Janet Fitchen's findings from the early 1980s confirm this pattern nationally.

2. It is difficult to estimate the number of people who access emergency food because EFPs are not required to keep detailed records.

Feeding America, which is an umbrella organization that represents food banks nationally, estimates these numbers by surveying their members. Though exact numbers are difficult to produce, the sheer number of providers and the increased numbers of clients they uniformly report confirm a marked increase in demand.

3. Since 2014, several other states with Republican governors have voluntarily foregone these waivers, and since 2016, falling unemployment rates across the country have meant these work requirements are being enforced more broadly.

4. It is difficult to know exactly how many people are given WEP assignments in nonprofit organizations. HRA keeps statistics on the number of WEP workers in city agencies. In September of 2013 there were 10,549 participants assigned to WEP according to *the Mayor's Management Report*. Of these 5,178 were assigned to a city agency. The other 5,371 were "housed in the MTA and non-profit organizations." Community Voices Heard, a welfare rights organization, estimates that there are at least one thousand individuals assigned to nonprofits at any given time. But, as with the number of WEP workers in particular city agencies, these numbers most likely fluctuate over time.

CHAPTER SIX. NO FREE LUNCH: THE LIMITS
OF FOOD ASSISTANCE AS A PUBLIC HEALTH
INTERVENTION

1. There is an enduring belief in the United States that the solution to public health problems tied to diet can be addressed through nutrition education. As Meagan Carney shows in her book *The Unending Hunger*, (2015) emergency food providers in California have made nutrition education a priority. But as Carney demonstrates and as Stephanie's experience shows, many low-income families are acutely aware of the health implications of the food they eat. They simply do not have any other options because of the financial and logistical constraints they face.

2. HPNAP is a grant program run by New York State that provides funds to emergency food providers that can be used to purchase food for distribution.

CHAPTER SEVEN. ENDING HUNGER, ADDRESSING THE CRISIS

1. An application for potential WEP employers confirms this view, stating, "The purpose of the Work Experience Program (WEP) is to place public assistance (PA) recipients in Work Experience assignments at government and not-for-profit agencies. Work Experience assignments provide PA recipients with an opportunity to learn about the world of work while they perform tasks that are useful to the sponsoring agencies." Nowhere in these documents does it mention any obligation on the part of the sponsoring agencies to consider hiring WEP employees or offer them regular employment.

POSTSCRIPT: THE RIGHT TO FOOD IN THE TRUMP ERA

1. For a review of the evidence that TANF work requirements fail to reduce poverty, see Ladonna Pavetti's (2016) report *Work Requirements Don't Cut Poverty, Evidence Shows*, published by the Center for Budget and Policy Priorities.

BIBLIOGRAPHY

Adad-Santos, Alexander. 2013. "Instead of Raises, McDonald's Tells Workers to Sign Up for Food Stamps." *The Atlantic*, October 24, 2013, Businesss.

Adams, Vincanne. 2012. "The Other Road to Serfdom: Recovery by the Market and the Affect Economy in New Orleans." *Public Culture* 24 (1): 185–216.

Alexander, Michelle. 2010. *The New Jim Crow: Mass Incarceration in the Age of Colorblindness*. New York: The New Press.

Allison, Anne. 2012. "Ordinary Refugees: Social Precarity and Soul in 21st Century Japan." *Anthropological Quarterly* 85 (2): 345–70.

American Public Health Association (APHA). 2013. "Public Health Takes on Obesity: A Route to Better Health."Infographic. http://uat.apha.org/news-and-media/multimedia/infographics/obesity-infographic

Appadurai, A. 1981. "Gastro-Politics in Hindu South Asia." *American Ethnologist* 8 (3): 494–511.

Ball, Molly. 2012. "What Obama Really Did to Welfare Reform." *The Atlantic*, August 9.

Barnhill, Anne. 2011. "Impact and Ethics of Excluding Sweetened Beverages from the SNAP Program." *American Journal of Public Health* 101 (11): 2037–43.

Beckett, Katherine, and Bruce Western. 2001. "Governing Social Marginality: Welfare, Incarceration, and the Transformation of State Policy." *Punishment and Society* 3 (1): 43–59.

Bellafante, Ginia. 2013. "A Mayor Who Puts Wall Street First." *New York Times*, August 16.

Ben-Shalom, Yonatan, Robert A. Moffitt, and John Karl Scholz. 2011. *An Assessment of the Effectiveness of Anti-Poverty Programs in the United States.* Washington, DC: National Bureau of Economic Research.

Berlant, Lauren. 2007. "Slow Death (Sovereignty, Obesity, Lateral Agency)." *Critical Inquiry* 33 (4): 754–80.

Bhattacharya, Tithi. 2013. "What Is Social Reproduction Theory." *Socialist Worker*, September 10, 2013.

Bitler, Marianne P., Hilary Hoynes, Christopher Jencks, and Bruce D. Meyers. 2010. "The State of the Social Safety Net in the Post-Welfare Reform Era." *Brookings Papers on Economic Activity* (Fall): 71–147.

Blackstock, Nelson. 1975. *Cointelpro: The FBI's Secret War on Political Freedom*. Atlanta, GA: Pathfinder Press.

Blank, Rebecca, and Brian Kovak. 2008. "Helping Disconnected Single Mothers." Policy brief, April 10. National Poverty Center. http://www.npc.umich.edu/publications/policy_briefs/brief10/policy_brief10.pdf.

Bolen, Ed, Dottie Rosenbaum, Stacy Dean, and Brynne Keith-Jennings. 2016. "More Than 500,000 Adults Will Lose SNAP Benefits in 2016 as Waivers Expire." Center on Budget and Policy Priorities. https://www.cbpp.org/research/food-assistance/more-than-500000-adults-will-lose-snap-benefits-in-2016-as-waivers-expire.

Bosman, Julie. 2009. "City Aids Homeless with One-Way Tickets Home." *New York Times*, July 28.

Bourgois, Phillipe. 1996. *In Search of Respect: Selling Crack in El Barrio.* New York: Cambridge University Press.

———. 2011. "Lumpen Abuse: The Human Cost of Righteous Neoliberalism." *City and Society* 23 (1): 2–12.

Brash, Julian. 2011. *Bloomberg's New York: Class and Governance in the Luxury City.* Athens: University of Georgia Press.

Brown, Wendy. 2015. *Undoing the Demos: Neoliberalism's Stealth Revolution.* Brooklyn, NY: Zone Books.

Brynjolfsson, Erik, and Andrew McAfee. 2011. *Race against the Machine: How the Digital Revolution Is Accelerating Innovation, Driving Productivity, and Irreversibly Transforming Employment and the Economy.* Lexington, MA: Digital Frontier Press.

Budig, Michelle. 2014. *The Fatherhood Bonus and the Motherhood Penalty: Parenthood and the Gender Gap in Pay.* Third Way, September 2. https://www.thirdway.org/report/the-fatherhood-bonus-and-the-mother hood-penalty-parenthood-and-the-gender-gap-in-pay.

Bureau of Labor Statistics (BLS). 2010. "Labor Force Participation Rates among Mothers." https://www.bls.gov/opub/ted/2010/ted_20100507 .htm?view_full.

———. 2016. "Labor Force Statistics from the Current Population Survey." https://www.bls.gov/cps/.

———. 2018. "The Employment Situation—February 2018." https://www.bls.gov/bls/news-release/empsit.htm.

Caldwell, Melissa. 2004. *Not by Bread Alone: Social Support in the New Russia.* Berkely: University of California Press.

Cardwell, Diane. 2003. "Mayor Says New York Is Worth the Cost." *New York Times,* January 8.

Carney, Megan. 2015. *The Unending Hunger: Tracing Women's Food Insecurity across Borders.* Oakland: University of California Press.

Caro, Robert. 1974. *The Power Broker: Robert Moses and the Fall of New York.* New York: Alfred A. Knopf.

Castner, L., and J. Henke. 2011. "Benefit Redemption Patterns in the Supplemental Nutrition Assistance Program." Food and Nutriton Service Office of Research and Analysis: USDA. https://www.fns.usda.gov /snap/benefit-redemption-patterns-supplemental-nutrition-assistance -program.

Centers for Disease Control and Prevention (CDC). 2017. *National Diabetes Statistics Report, 2017.* Atlanta, GA: Centers for Disease Control and Prevention.

———. 2018. "High Blood Pressure Fact Sheet." https://www.cdc .gov/dhdsp/data_statistics/fact_sheets/fs_bloodpressure.htm.

Chan, Sewell. 2006. "Mayor Overrules 2 Aides Seeking Food Stamp Shift". *New York Times,* April 18.

Chappell, M. Jahi. 2018. *Beggining to End Hunger: Food and the Environment in Belo Horizonte, Brazil, and Beyond.* Berkely: University of California Press.

Chesney-Lind, Meda. 1995. *The Female Offender.* Thousand Oaks, CA: Sage.

Chilton, Mariana, and Jenny Rabinowich. 2012. "Toxic Stress and Child Hunger over the Life Course: Three Case Studies." *Journal of Applied Research on Children: Informing Policy for Children at Risk* 3 (1).

Chilton, Mariana, and Donald Rose. 2009. "A Rights Based Approach to Food Insecurity in the United States." *American Journal of Public Health* 99 (7): 1203–11.

Clement, Scott. 2017. "Hard-Working Taxpayers Don't Support Big Cuts to Food Stamps, It Turns Out." *Washington Post,* May 25.

Coleman-Jensen, Alisha, Matthew Rabbitt, Christian Gregory, and Anita Singh. 2017. *Household Food Security in the United States in 2016.* Edited by United States Department of Agriculture. Washington, DC: USDA Economic Research Service.

Colen, Shellee. 1995. "Like a Mother to Them: Stratified Reproduction and West Indian Childcare Workers and Employers in New York." In *Conceiving the New World Order: The Global Politics of Reproduction,* edited by Faye D. Ginsburg and Rayna Rapp, 78–102. Berkeley: University of California Press.

Collins, Jane Lou. 2008. "The Specter of Slavery: Workfare and the Economic Citizenship of Poor Women." In *New Landscapes of Inequality: Neoliberalism and the Erosion of Democracy in America,* edited by M. diLeonardo, Jane Lou Collins, and Brett Williams, 131–52. Santa Fe, NM: School for Advanced Research Press.

Collins, Jane Lou, and Victoria Mayer. 2010. *Both Hands Tied: Welfare Reform and the Race to the Bottom in the Low-Wage Labor Market.* Chicago: University of Chicago Press.

Combahee River Collective. 1977. "The Combahee River Collective Statement." http://circuitous.org/scraps/combahee.html.

Coontz, Stephanie. 1992. *The Way We Never Were.* New York: Basic Books.

Council of Economic Advisors. 2016. *The Long-Term Decline in Prime-Age Male Labor Force Participation.* Washington, DC: Executive Office

of the President of the United States. https://obamawhitehouse
.archives.gov/sites/default/files/page/files/20160620_cea_primeage
_male_lfp.pdf.

Counihan, Carole, and Steven Kaplan. 1998. *Food and Gender: Identity
and Power.* Newark, NJ: Harwood Academic.

Cox, Aimee Meredith. 2015. *Shapeshifters: Black Girls and the Choreography
of Citizenship.* Durham, NC: Duke University Press.

Crenson, Matthew, and Benjamin Ginsberg. 2002. *Downsizing Democracy: How America Sidelined Its Citizens and Privatized Its Public.* Balti-
more, MD: Johns Hopkins University Press.

Cruikshank, Barbara. 1999. *The Will to Empower: Democratic Citizens and
Other Subjects.* Ithaca, NY: Cornell University Press.

Cunnyngham, Karen. 2018. *Trends in Supplemental Nutrition Assistance
Program Participation Rates: Fiscal Year 2010 to Fiscal Year 2016.* Washington, DC: USDA Food and Nutrition Service. https://fns-prod
.azureedge.net/sites/default/files/snap/Trends2010-2016.pdf.

Danese, Andrea, Terrie Moffitt, and HonaLee Harrington. 2009.
"Adverse Childhood Experiences and Adult Risk Factors for Age-
Related Disease." *JAMA Pediatrics* 163 (12): 1135–43.

Darmon, Nicole, and Adam Drewnoski. 2008. "Does Social Class Pre-
dict Diet Quality?" *The American Journal of Clinical Nutrition* 87:
1107–17.

Davis, Dana Ain et al. 2002. *The Impact of Welfare Reform on Two Communities in New York City.* New York State Scholar Practitioner Team,
CUNY Graduate Center PhD Program in Anthropology.

Deaton, Angus. 2018. "The U.S. Can No Longer Hide From Its Deep
Poverty Problem." *New York Times,* January 24, 2018.

Dehavenon, Anna Lou. 1995. "Hunger and Homelessness in New York
City." In *Science, Materialism, and the Study of Culture,* edited by Martin F. Murray and Maxine Margolis. Gainsville: University Press
of Florida.

Delaney, Arthur, and Emily Swanson. 2013. "Food Stamp Cut Popular
with Republican Voters." *Huffington Post,* November 15. https://
www.huffpost.com/entry/food-stamp-cut_n_4276208?guccounter
=1&guce_referrer=aHR0cHM6Ly93d3cuZ29vZ2xlLmNvbS8&guce
_referrer_sig=AQAAAJxk1E1iigwO5k4RWWr8ypaazMoNtooUkD

Nz29sLSdo2LUJ510rl5f439n-z-hP6WcMZUDA5fJlfgGBfUFzwhvE
HKt-31BIYPr5NovPKvdC7fmur1-HfdERKEKLdJmurPpivPcrpPzX
Pmu18vIW25B97kQVl8Btr
blNcyYTpFS7j.

DeParle, Jason, and Robert Gebeloff. 2010. "Once Stigmatized, Food Stamps Find Acceptance." *New York Times*, February 10, Politics.

Desmond, Matthew. 2015. "Unaffordable America, Poverty, Housing and Eviction." In *Fast Focus*. Madison: University of Wisconsin, Institute for Research on Poverty.

———. 2016. *Evicted: Poverty and Profit in the American City*. New York: Crown Publishers.

Devault, Marjorie. 1991. *Feeding the Family: The Social Organization of Caring as Gendered Work*. Chicago: Chicago University Press.

Dickinson, Maggie. 2016. "Working for Food Stamps: Economic Citizenship and the Post-Fordist Welfare State." *American Ethnologist* 43 (2): 270–81.

———. 2013. "Cooking Up a Revolution: Food as a Democratic Tactic at Occupy Wall Street." *Food, Culture and Society* 16 (3): 359–65.

DiTomaso, Nancy. 2013. *The American Non-Dilemma: Racial Inequality without Racism*. New York: Russell Sage Foundation.

Dreze, Jean, and A. Sen. 1989. *Hunger and Public Action*. Oxford: Clarendon Press.

Duncan, Greg J., and P. Chase-Lansdale. 2002. *For Better and for Worse: Welfare Reform and the Well-Being of Children and Families*. New York: Russell Sage Foundation.

Dunlea, Mark. 2009. *Evaluating a Decade of Welfare Reform in New York State*. New York: Hunger Action Network.

Edin, K., and H. Luke Shaefer. 2016. *$2.00 A Day: Living on Almost Nothing in America*. New York: Mariner Books.

Edin, Kathryn, and Timothy Nelson. 2013. *Doing the Best I Can: Fatherhood in the Inner City*. Berkley: University of California Press.

Edsall, Thomas, and Mary Edsall. 1992. *Chain Reaction: The Impact of Race, Rights and Taxes on American Politics*. New York: Norton.

Elwood, Sarah, and Victoria Lawson. 2018. "(Un)Thinkable Poverty Politics." In *Relational Poverty Politcs: Forms, Struggles and Possibilities*, edited by Victoria Lawson and Sarah Elwood. Athens: University of Georgia Press.

Errington, Frederick, Tatsuro Fujikura, and Deborah Gewertz. 2012. "Instant Noodles as an Antifriction Device: Making the BOP with PPP in PNG." *Amercian Anthropologist* 114 (1): 19–31.

Fantasia, R. 1995. "Fast Food in France." *Theory Soc.* 24 (2): 201–43.

Federici, Sylvia. 2012. "The Reproduction of Labor Power in the Global Economy and the Unfinished Feminist Revolution." In *Revolution at Point Zero: Housework, Reproduction and Feminist Struggle*, edited by Sylvia Federici. Brooklyn, NY: Common Notions.

Feeding America. 2018. "The Emergency Food Assistance Program (TEFAP)." Feeding America. Accessed May 15, 2018. http://www.feedingamerica.org/take-action/advocate/federal-hunger-relief-programs/the-emergency-food-assistance-program.html.

Ferguson, James. 2015. *Give a Man a Fish: Reflections on the New Politics of Distribution.* Durham, NC: Duke University Press.

Fernandes, Sujatha. 2007. "Barrio Women and Popular Politics in Chavez's Venezuela." *Latin American Politics and Society* 49 (3): 97–127.

Fitchen, JM. 1988. "Hunger, Malnutrition, and Poverty in the Contemporary United States: Some Observations on Their Social and Cultural Context." *Food and Foodways* 2: 309–33.

Ford, Martin. 2015. *Rise of the Robots: Technology and the Threat of a Jobless Future.* New York: Basic Books.

Fox, Cybelle. 2012. *Three Worlds of Relief: Race, Immigration and the American Welfare State from the Progressive Era to the New Deal.* Princeton, NJ: Princeton University Press.

Frase, Peter. 2016. *Four Futures: Life after Capitalism.* Jacobin Series. New York: Verso.

Fraser, Nancy, and Linda Gordon. 1994. "A Genealogy of Dependency: Tracing a Keyword of the U.S. Welfare State." *Signs* 19 (2): 309–36.

Germani, Clara. 1981. "Reagan Picks Taskforce to Foster Volunteerism." *Christian Science Monitor,* October 6.

Gilens, Martin. 1999. *Why Americans Hate Welfare: Race, Media, and the Politics of Anti-Poverty Policy.* Chicago: Chicago University Press.

Gilmore, Ruth Wilson. 2007. *Golden Gulag: Prisons, Surplus, Crisis and Opposition in Globalizing California.* Berkely: University of California Press.

———. 2009. "In the Shadow of the Shadow State." In *The Revolution Will Not Be Funded,* edited by INCITE!, 41–52. Boston: South End Press.

Glenn, Evelyn Nakano. 2002. *Unequal Freedom: How Race and Gender Shaped American Citizenship and Labor.* Cambridge, MA: Harvard University Press.

Gunderson, Craig, Brent Kreider, and John Pepper. 2018. "Reconstructing the Supplemental Nutrition Assistance Program to More Effectively Alleviate Food Insecurity in the United States." *The Russell Sage Foundation Journal of the Social Sciences* 4 (2): 113–30.

Gupta, Akhil. 2012. *Red Tape: Bureaucracy, Structural Violence and Poverty in India.* Durham, NC: Duke University Press.

Guthman, Julie. 2011. *Weighing In: Obesity, Food Justice, and the Limits of Capitalism.* Berkeley: University of California Press.

Hacker, Jacob. 2006. *The Great Risk Shift: The Assault on American Jobs, Families, Health Care and Retirement (And How You Can Fight Back).* New York: Oxford University Press.

Halloran, Liz. 2013. "Lobster Boy Looms Large in Food Stamp Debate." *NPR, Its All Politics.* http://www.npr.org/sections/itsallpolitics/2013 /09/19/223796325/lobster-boy-looms-large-in-food-stamp-debate.

Hancock, Ange-Marie. 2004. *The Politics of Disgust: The Public Identity of the Welfare Queen.* New York: New York University Press.

Haney-Lopez, Ian. 2014. *Dog Whistle Politics: How Coded Racial Appeals Reinvented Racism and Wrecked the Middle Class.* New York: Oxford University Press.

Harrington, Michael. 1962. *The Other America: Poverty in the United States.* New York: Simon and Schuster.

Harrington, Mona. 2000. *Care and Equality: Inventing a New Family Politics.* New York: Routledge.

Harvey, David. 2000. *Spaces of Hope.* Berkeley: University of California Press.

Haskins, Ron. 2006. "Interview: Welfare Reform, 10 Years Later." *On the Record,* August 24. Brookings Institute. https://www.brookings .edu/on-the-record/interview-welfare-reform-10-years-later/.

Hinton, Elizabeth. 2016. *From the War on Poverty to the War on Crime: The Making of Mass Incarceration in America.* Cambridge, MA: Harvard University Press.

hooks, bell. 1984. *Feminist Theory: From Margin to Center.* New York: Routledge.

Hyatt, Susan Brin. 2001. "From Citizen to Volunteer: Neoliberal Governance and the Erasure of Poverty." In *The New Poverty Studies: The Ethnography of Power, Politics and Impoverished People in the United States,* edited by Judith Goode and Jeff Maskovsky. New York: New York University Press.

Independent Budget Office (IBO). 2008. "Most Food Stamp Recipients No Longer Also Welfare Recipients." Fiscal brief. https://ibo.nyc .ny.us/iboreports/Foodstamps.pdf.

Institute of Medicine and National Research Council. 2013. *Supplemental Nutrition Assistance Program: Examining the Evidence to Define Benefit Adequacy.* National Academy of Sciences. Washington, DC: Natiional Academies Press.

Jacobs-Huey, Lanita. 2008. "The Natives Are Gazing and Talking Back: Reviewing Problematics of Positionality, Voice, and Accountability among "Native" Anthropologists." *Amercian Anthropologist* 104 (3):791–804.

James, Selma. 2012. *Sex, Race and Class.* New York: PM Press. Original edition, 1974.

Joint Center for Housing Studies (JCHS). 2016. "Key Facts." *State of the Nation's Housing 2016.* Harvard University. https://thepowerisnow .com/wp-content/uploads/2016/09/State-of-the-Natioin-Housing -key-facts.pdf.

Julier, Alice. 2013. "The Political Economy of Obesity: The Fat Pay All." In *Food and Culture: A Reader,* edited by Carole Counihan and Penny Van Esterik, 546–62. New York: Routledge.

Kalleberg, Arne. 2011. *Good Jobs, Bad Jobs: The Rise of Polarized and Precarious Employment Systems in the United States, 1970s to 2000s.* New York: Russell Sage Foundation.

Katz, Lawrence, and Alan Krueger. 2016. "The Rise and Nature of Alternative Work Arrangements in the United States, 1995–2015." Working paper no. 22667. National Bureau of Economic Research, March 29.

Katz, Michael. 1986. *In the Shadow of the Poorhouse: A Social History of Welfare in America*. New York: Basic Books.

———. 2001. *The Price of Citizenship: Redefining America's Welfare State*. New York: Metropolitan Books.

Katznelson, Ira. 2005. *When Affirmative Action Was White: The Untold History of Racial Inequality in Twentieth-Century America*. New York: W.W. Norton.

Kim, M., D. Berger, and T. Matte. 2006. *Diabetes in New York City: Public Health Burden and Disparities*. New York: New York City Department of Health and Mental Hygiene. https://www1.nyc.gov/assets/doh/downloads/pdf/epi/diabetes_chart_book.pdf.

Kingfisher, C. 1996. *Women in the American Welfare Trap*. Philadelphia: University of Pennsylvania Press.

Kleinfield, N.R. 2006. "Diabetes and Its Awful Toll Quietly Emerge as a Crisis." *New York Times*, January 9.

Koible, William Guillaume, and Triada Stampas. 2016. "Still Scaling the Hunger Cliff: Need at NYC Food Pantries and Soup Kitchens." Research brief. Food Bank of New York City. http://1giqgs400j4 83ok22r3m4wqg-wpengine.netdna-ssl.com/wp-content/uploads/2016/_Still-Scaling-Hunger-Cliff_LegislativeBreakfast_ResearchBrief_11_19.pdf.

Kornbluh, Felicia. 2007. *The Battle for Welfare Rights: Politics and Poverty in Modern America*. Philadelphia: University of Pennsylvania Press.

———. 2015. "Food as a Civil Right: Hunger, Work and Welfare in the South after the Civil Rights Act." *Labor: Studies in Working Class History of the Americas* 12 (1–2): 135–58.

Kotz, Nick. 1979. *Hunger in America: The Federal Response*. New York: The Field Foundation.

Krinsky, J. 2007. *Free Labor: Workfare and the Contested Language of Neoliberalism*. Chicago: University of Chicago Press.

Lambert, Susan. 2008. "Passing the Buck: Labor Flexibility Practices That Transfer Risk onto Hourly Workers." *Human Relations* 61 (9): 1203–27.

Leacock, Eleanor. 1987. "Theory and Ethics in Applied Urban Anthropology." In *Cities of the United States: Studies in Urban Anthropology*, edited by Leith Mullings, 317–36. New York: Columbia University Press.

Lee, Richard Borsay. 1979. *The !Kung San: Men, Women and Work in a Foraging Society.* New York: Cambridge University Press.

Lee, Tina. 2010. "Stratified Reproduction and Definitions of Child Neglect: State Practices and Parents' Responses." PhD diss., Department of Anthropology, CUNY Graduate Center.

Lein, Laura. 2007. *Life after Welfare Reform and the Persistence of Poverty.* Austin: University of Texas Press.

Lein, Laura, and Kathryn Edin. 1997. *Making Ends Meet: How Single Mothers Survive Welfare and Low-Wage Work.* New York: Russell Sage Foundation.

Levenstein, Harvey. 1993. *Paradox of Plenty: A Social History of Eating in Modern America.* New York: Oxford University Press.

Lohnes, Joshua, and Bradley Wilson. 2018. "Bailing out the food banks? Hunger relief, food waste and crisis in Central Appalachia." *Environment and Planning A: Economy and Space* 50(2) 350–369.

Lubrano, Alfred. 2017. "'Pimping Out' Drug Addicts for Cash." *Philadelphia Inquirer,* June 1. http://www.philly.com/philly/health /addiction/Philadelphia_exploited_heroin_addicts_recovery_hous es_treatment_centers_kickbacks_Medicaid.html.

Malbi, James, Rhoda Cohen, Frank Potter, and Zhanyun Zhao. 2010. *Hunger in America 2010: National Report Prepared for Feeding America.* Mathmatica Policy Research. Princeton, NJ: Feeding America. https:// www.mathematica-mpr.com/our-publications-and-findings/publica tions/hunger-in-america-2010-national-report-prepared-for-feeding -america.

Mares, Teresa Marie. 2013. "Here We Have the Food Bank": Latino/a Immigration and the Contradictions of Emergency Food." *Food and Foodways* 21 (1): 1–21.

Maskovsky, Jeff, and Judith Goode. 2001. "Introduction." In *The New Poverty Studies: The Ethnography of Power, Politics and Impoverished People in the United States,* edited by Judith Goode and Jeff Maskovsky. New York: New York University Press.

Maskovsky, Jeff, and Sandra Morgen. 2003. "The Anthropology of Welfare 'Reform': New Perspectives on U.S. Urban Poverty in the Post-Welfare Era." *Annual Review of Anthropology* 32: 315–38.

Massey, Douglas, and Nancy Denton. 1993. *American Apartheid: Segregation and the Making of the Underclass*. Cambridge, MA: Harvard Univerisity Press.

McGovern, James. 2014. "The Costly Problem of Hunger." *Congressional Record* 160, no. 9 (January 15): H230–H231. https://www.congress.gov/congressional-record/2014/01/15/house-section/article/H230-1.

Mead, Lawrence. 1986. *Beyond Entitlement: The Social Obligations of Citizenship*. New York: The Free Press.

Messer, Ellen, and Marc Cohen. 2007. *The Human Right to Food as a U.S. Nutrition Concern, 1976–2006*. Washington DC: International Food Policy Research Institute. http://www.ifpri.org/publication/human -right-food-us-nutrition-concern-1976-2006.

Millar, Kathleen. 2008. "Making Trash into Treasure: Struggles for Autonomy on a Brazilian Garbage Dump." *Anthropology of Work Review* 29 (2): 25–34.

Mintz, Sidney. 1995. *Sweetness and Power*. New York: Penguin.

Moffitt, Robert A. 2015. "The Deserving Poor, the Family, and the U.S. Welfare System." *Demography* 52: 729–49.

Molé, Noelle. 2010. "Precarious Subjects: Anticipating Neoliberalism in Northern Italy's Workplace." *American Anthropologist* 112 (1): 38–53.

Morgen, Sandra. 2001. "The Agency of Welfare Workers: Negotiating Devolution, Privatization and Self-Sufficiency." *Amercian Anthropology* 103 (3): 747–61.

Muehlebach, Andrea. 2011. "On Affective Labor in Post-Fordist Italy." *Cultural Anthropology* 26 (1): 59–82.

———. 2012. *The Moral Neoliberal: Welfare and Citizenship in Italy*. Chicago: University of Chicago Press.

Mullings, Leith. 1995. "Households Headed by Women: The Politics of Race, Class and Gender." In *Conceiving the New World Order: The Global Politics of Reproduction*, edited by Faye D. Ginsburg and Rayna Rapp. Berkeley: University of California Press.

———. 1997. "Uneven Development: Class, Race and Gender in the United States Before 1900." In *On Our Own Terms: Race, Class and Gender in the Lives of African American Women*, edited by Leith Mullings. New York: Routledge.

Murray, Charles. 1984. *Losing Ground*. New York: Basic Books.

Nadasen, P. 2004. *Welfare Warriors: The Welfare Rights Movement in the United States.* New York: Routledge.

Narayan, Kirin. 1993. "How Native Is a "Native" Anthropologist?" *Amercian Anthropologist* 95 (3): 671–86.

National Employment Law Project (NELP). 2014. *Tracking the Low-Wage Recovery: Industry Employment and Wages.* New York: National Employment Law Project. https://www.nelp.org/publication/tracking-the -low-wage-recovery-industry-employment-wages/.

Nelson, Alondra. 2012. *Body and Soul: The Black Panther Party and the Fight against Discrimination.* Minneapolis: University of Minnesota Press.

Neubuck, Kenneth, and Nathan Cazenave. 2001. *Welfare Racism: Playing the Race Card against America's Poor.* New York: Routledge.

Newman, Katherine. 1999. *No Shame in My Game: The Working Poor in the Inner City.* New York: Alfred A. Knopf.

—. 2001. "Hard Times on 125th Street: Harlem's Poor Confront Welfare Reform." *American Anthropologist* 103 (3): 762–78.

O'Brien, Matt. 2018. "What's Wrong Here? Unemployment Is Below 4 Percent, but Wage Growth Is Still Lousy." *Washington Post,* May 4.

Pappas, Gregory. 1989. *The Magic City: Unemployment in a Working-Class Community.* Ithaca, NY: Cornell University Press.

Patel, Raj. 2012. "Survival Pending Revolution: What the Black Panthers Can Teach the US Food Movement." *Food First Backgrounder* 18 (2).

Paul, Mark, William Darity, and Darrick Hamilton. 2018. *The Federal Job Guarantee: A Policy to Achieve Permanent Full Employment.* Washington, DC: Center on Budget and Policy Priorities. https://www .cbpp.org/research/full-employment/the-federal-job-guarantee-a -policy-to-achieve-permanent-full-employment.

Pavetti, Ladonna. 2016. "Work Requirements Don't Cut Poverty, Evidence Shows." Washington DC: Center for Budget and Policy Priorities. https://www.cbpp.org/research/poverty-and-inequality/work -requirements-dont-cut-poverty-evidence-shows.

Peck, J. 2001. *Workfare States.* New York: Guilford Press.

Peck, J., N. Theodore, and N. Brenner. 2009. "Postneoliberalism and Its Malcontents." *Antipode* 41 (81): 94–116.

Philips, Nune. 2016. "How States Can Protect Workers with Irregular Schedules from Losing SNAP Benefits." Washington, DC: Center for Law and Social Policy. https://www.clasp.org/sites/default /files/public/resources-and-publications/publication-1/2016.10.18-A BAWD-Irregular-Schedules-FINAL.pdf.

Piven, Frances Fox. 2001. "Welfare Reform and the Economic and Cultural Reconstruction of Low-Wage Labor Markets." In *The New Poverty Studies: The Ethnography of Power, Politics and Impoverished People in the United States*, edited by Judith Goode and Jeff Maskovsky. New York: New York University Press.

Piven, Frances Fox, and Richard Cloward. 1979. *Poor People's Movements: Why They Succeed, How They Fail.* New York: Vintage Books.

———. 1993. *Regulating the Poor: The Functions of Public Welfare.* Updated ed. New York: Vintage Books.

Poppendieck, Janet. 1994. "Dilemmas of Emergency Food: A Guide for the Perplexed." *Agriculture and Human Values* (Fall): 69–76.

———. 1998. *Sweet Charity: Emergency Food and the End of Entitlement.* New York: Viking Press.

———. 2014. *Breadlines Knee Deep in Wheat: Food Assistance in the Great Depression.* Berkley: University of California Press.

Purser, Gretchen, and Brian Hennigan. 2017. "Cleaning Toilets for Jesus." *Jacobin*, June 30. https://www.jacobinmag.com/2017/06/work -to-welfare-unemployment-christian-right-jobs-for-life.

Quadagno, Jill. 1996. *The Color of Welfare: How Racism Undermined the War on Poverty.* New York: Oxford.

Quayle, Dan. 1992. Address to the Commonwealth Club of California. http://www.vicepresidentdanquayle.com/speeches_StandingFirm _CCC_1.html.

Ranci, Costanzo. 2001. "Democracy at Work: Social Participation in the 'Third Sector' in Italy." *Daedalus* 130 (3): 73–84.

Reese, Ashanté. 2018. "We Will Not Perish; We're Going to Keep Flourishing": Race, Food Access, and Geographies of Self-Reliance." *Antipode* 50 (2): 407–24.

Robertson, Nan. 1967. "Severe Hunger Found in Mississippi." *New York Times*, June 16.

Rocha, Cecilia, and Lara Lessa. 2010. "Urban Governance for Food Security: The Alternative Food System in Belo Horizonte, Brazil." *International Planning Studies* 14 (4): 389–400.

Ryan, Paul. 2012. "Paul Ryan's Speech to Values Voter Summit (Prepared Remarks)." *Washington Post*, September 14, https://www.wash ington post.com/politics/decision2012/paul-ryans-speech-to-values-voter -summit-prepared-remarks/2012/09/14/b8bb1070-fe83-11e1-8adc-4996 61afe377_story.html?utm_term=.cde8bbac28f1.

Sassen, Saskia. 1994. "The Informal Economy: Between New Developments and Old Regulations." *Yale Law Journal* 103 (8):2289–304.

———. 2014. *Expulsions: Brutality and Complexity in the Global Economy.* Cambridge, MA: Harvard University Press.

Scharff, Jagna. 1987. "The Underground Economy of a Poor Neighborhood." In *Cities of the United States*, edited by Leith Mullings. New York: Columbia University Press.

Schlosser, Eric. 2002. *Fast Food Nation: The Dark Side of the All-American Meal.* New York: Houghton Mifflin.

Schmitt, John. 2015. "Failing on Two Fronts: The U.S. Labor Market Since 2000." Washington, DC: Center for Economic and Policy Research, January. http://cepr.net/documents/failure-two-fronts-2015-01.pdf.

Seefeldt, Kristin. 2016. *Abandoned Families: Social Isolation in the Twenty-First Century.* New York: Russell Sage Foundation.

Shklar, Judith. 1998. *American Citizenship: The Quest for Inclusion.* Cambridge, MA: Harvard University Press.

Soss, Joe, Richard Fording, and Sanford Schram. 2011. *Disciplining the Poor: Neoliberal Paternalism and the Persistent Power of Race.* Chicago: University of Chicago Press.

Spence, Lester. 2015. *Knocking the Hustle: Against the Neoliberal Turn in Black Politics.* Brooklyn, NY: Punctum Books.

Stack, Carol B. 1974. *All Our Kin: Strategies for Survival in a Black Community.* New York: Harper and Row.

Standing, Guy. 2011. *The Precariat: The New Dangerous Class.* London: Bloomsbury Academic.

Strathern, Marilyn. 1988. *The Gender of the Gift: Problems with Women and Problems with Society in Melanesia.* Berkeley: University of California Press.

Stein, David. 2016. "This Nation Has Never Honestly Dealt with the Question of a Peacetime Economy": Coretta Scott King and the Struggle for a Nonviolent Economy in the 1970s." *Souls* 18 (1): 80–105.

Super, David A. 2004. "The Quiet "Welfare" Revolution: Resurrecting the Food Stamp Program in the Wake of the 1996 Welfare Law." *New York University Law Review* 79 (October).

Taylor, Keeanga-Yamahatta, ed. 2017. *How We Get Free: Black Feminism and the Combahee River Collective.* Chicago: Haymarket Books.

Tcherneva, Pavlina. 2018. "The Job Guarantee." Levy Economics Institute Working Paper Collection. http://www.levyinstitute.org /pubs/wp_902.pdf.

Thistle, Susan. 2006. *From Marriage to the Market: The Transformation of Women's Lives and Work.* Berkeley: University of California Press.

Ticktin, Miriam. 2006. "Where Ethics and Politics Meet: The Violence of Humanitarianism in France." *American Ethnologist* 33 (1): 33–49.

Tronto, Joan C. 2013. *Caring Democracy: Markets, Equality and Justice.* New York: New York University Press.

US Department of Agricuture (USDA). 2007. The Low-Cost, Moderate-Cost and Liberal Food Plans, 2007. edited by Center for Nutrition and Policy Promotion. https://fns-prod.azureedge.net/sites /default/files/usda_food_plans_cost_of_food/FoodPlans2007Admin Report.pdf.

———. 2013. "USDA and EPA Launch U.S. Food Waste Challenge." Press release, June 4. https://www.usda.gov/media/press-releases /2013/06/04/usda-and-epa-launch-us-food-waste-challenge.

———. 2017. State Options Report: Supplemental Nutrition Assistance Program. edited by Food and Nutrition Service. Washington DC: United States Department of Agriculture. https://fns-prod.azur eedge.net/sites/default/files/snap/13-State_Options-revised.pdf.

———. 2018. *SNAP National Level Annual Summary.* Washington DC: United States Department of Agriculture. https://www.fns.usda .gov/pd/supplemental-nutrition-assistance-program-snap.

Van Esterik, Penny. 1999. "Right to Food; Right to Feed; Right to Be Fed: The Intersection of Women's Rights and the Right to Food." *Agriculture and Human Values* 16: 225–32.

Wacquant, Loïc J. D. 2009. *Punishing the Poor: The Neoliberal Government of Social Insecurity, Politics, History, and Culture.* Durham, NC: Duke University Press.

Walley, Christine. 2010. "Deindustrializing Chicago: A Daughter's Story." In *The Insecure American: How We Got Here and What We Should Do about It,* edited by Hugh Gusterson and Catherine Besteman. Berkeley: University of California Press.

Watkins-Hayes, Celeste. 2009. *The New Welfare Bureaucrats: Entanglements of Race, Class and Policy Reform.* Chicago: Universitiy of Chicago Press.

Weeks, Kathi. 2011. *The Problem with Work.* Durham, NC: Duke University Press.

West, Guida. 1981. *The National Welfare Rights Movement: The Social Protest of Poor Women.* New York: Praeger.

Western, Bruce. 2001. "Incarceration, Unemployment and Inequality." *Focus* 21 (Spring 2001): 32–36.

White, Monica. 2011. "D-Town Farm: African American Resistance to Food Insecurity and the Transformation of Detriot." *Environmental Pracice* 13 (4).

Wienfield, Nancy, Gregory Mills, Christine Borger, Maeve Gearing, Theodore Mcaluso, Jill Montaquila, and Sheila Zedlewski. 2014. *Hunger in America.* Chicago: Feeding America. http://help.feedingamerica .org/HungerInAmerica/hunger-in-america-2014-full-report.pdf.

Williams, Raymond. 1976. *Keywords: A Vocabulary of Culture and Society.* New York: Oxford University Press.

Wilson, Claire, and Brian Estes. 2014. *Examining the Growth of the Zero-Income SNAP Caseload: Characteristics, Circumstances, and Dynamics of Zero-Income SNAP Participants.* Washington, DC: USDA Food and Nutrtion Service. https://fns-prod.azureedge.net/sites/default/files /ops/ZeroIncome-Vol1.pdf.

Wolkwitz, Kari. 2007. *Trends in Food Stamp Program Participation Rates: 1999 to 2005.* Alexandria, VA: United States Department of Agriculture. https://www.fns.usda.gov/snap/trends-food-stamp-program -participation-rates-1999-2005.

Woodburn, James. 1998. "Sharing Is Not a Form of Exchange": An Analysis of Property Sharing in Immediate-Return Hunter-Gatherer

Societies." In *Property Relations: Renewing an Anthropological Tradition*, edited by C. M. Hann. New York: Cambridge University Press.

Ziliak, James P. 2016. "Modernizing SNAP Benefits." The Hamilton Project, Brookings Institute, May 20. http://www.hamiltonproject.org/papers/modernizing_snap_benefits.

INDEX

CALIFORNIA STUDIES IN FOOD AND
CULTURE

Darra Goldstein, Editor

Founded in 1893,
UNIVERSITY OF CALIFORNIA PRESS
publishes bold, progressive books and journals
on topics in the arts, humanities, social sciences,
and natural sciences—with a focus on social
justice issues—that inspire thought and action
among readers worldwide.

The UC PRESS FOUNDATION
raises funds to uphold the press's vital role
as an independent, nonprofit publisher, and
receives philanthropic support from a wide
range of individuals and institutions—and from
committed readers like you. To learn more, visit
ucpress.edu/supportus.